KETO DIET
COOKBOOK FOR BEGINNERS

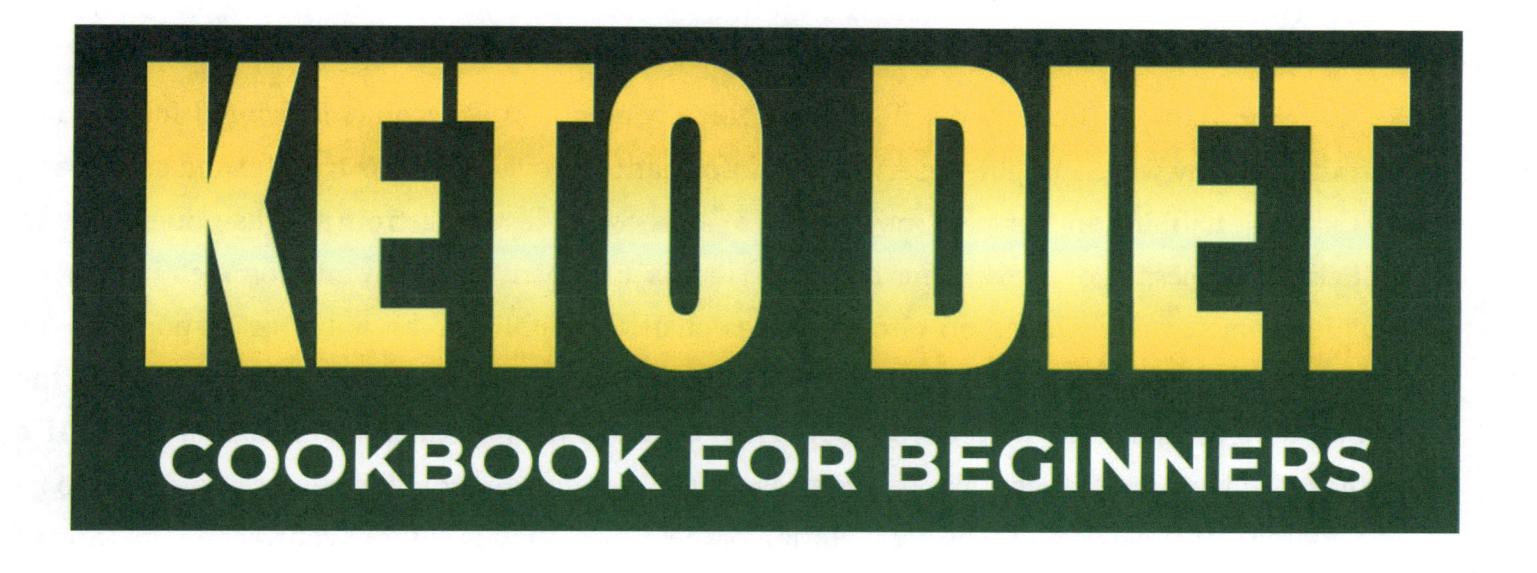

BUDGET-FRIENDLY, EASY, AND DELICIOUS LOW-CARB, LOW-SUGAR RECIPES READY IN MINUTES! INCLUDES A 28-DAY MEAL PLAN TO LOSE WEIGHT EFFORTLESSLY AND TRANSFORM YOUR HEALTH

Gertraud Kron

© Copyright 2025 by Gertraud Kron - All rights reserved.

This document is intended to provide accurate and reliable information regarding the subject matter discussed.

Reproduction, duplication, or distribution of this document in electronic or printed form is not permitted in any way. All rights reserved. The information provided here is truthful and consistent, so that any liability, in terms of negligence or otherwise, resulting from the use or misuse of guidelines, processes, or instructions contained in this document lies solely and completely with the recipient and reader. Under no circumstances shall the publisher be liable or responsible for compensation, damages, or financial losses that are directly or indirectly attributable to the information contained herein. All copyrights not owned by the publisher belong to their respective authors. The information contained herein is provided for informational purposes only and is to be considered universally valid. The presentation of the information is without contract or any form of warranty promise. The trademarks used are employed without permission, and the publication of the trademark is without the permission or endorsement of the trademark owner. All trademarks and brands in this book are used for clarification purposes only and belong to the owners themselves, who are not affiliated with this document.

Chapter 1: Introduction

Welcome to the "Ketogenic Diet Recipe Book XXL," your comprehensive guide to the world of ketogenic dieting. This book is designed to provide you not only with a collection of delicious recipes but also with a deep understanding of the principles and benefits of the ketogenic diet. Whether you are new to keto or looking to expand your existing knowledge, this book offers you the tools and information you need to achieve your health and wellness goals.

What is the Ketogenic Diet?

The ketogenic diet, often simply referred to as "keto," is a nutritional plan based on very low carbohydrate intake, moderate protein intake, and high fat intake. This approach leads the body to enter a metabolic state called ketosis, where fat is used as the primary energy source instead of glucose. The switch to fat burning instead of carbohydrate burning has numerous health benefits and is the main reason many people opt for a ketogenic diet.

Principles of the Ketogenic Diet

- **Carbohydrate Reduction:** To enter ketosis, the ketogenic diet reduces carbohydrate intake to typically below 50 grams per day, sometimes even below 20 grams. This drastic reduction forces the body to switch its energy source.
- **Fat as the Main Energy Source:** Fat makes up the majority of daily calorie intake, often 70% to 80%. By switching to fat as the main energy source, the body becomes more efficient at burning fat.
- **Moderate Protein Intake:** Protein is consumed in moderate amounts to preserve muscle mass without disrupting ketosis. Too much protein can be converted into glucose, which could kick the body out of ketosis.

Benefits of the Ketogenic Diet

- **Weight Loss:** Many people experience rapid weight loss on the keto diet, primarily through reduced insulin levels and improved fat burning.
- **Improved Energy and Concentration:** After overcoming the initial transition, many report an increase in energy and clearer mental focus.
- **Blood Sugar Control:** The ketogenic diet can help stabilize blood sugar levels, which is particularly beneficial for people with type 2 diabetes.
- **Reduction of Inflammation:** Some research suggests that the keto diet can reduce inflammation in the body, leading to improvement in certain chronic diseases.
- **Heart Health:** When done correctly, the keto diet can reduce the risk of heart disease by improving factors such as body weight, blood sugar, and cholesterol levels.

Challenges and Considerations While the ketogenic diet offers many potential benefits, it is not suitable for everyone and can lead to challenges if not done properly. Common issues include keto flu-like symptoms during the initial phase, nutrient deficiencies, and difficulty maintaining the diet due to its restrictions. It is important to consult a doctor or nutritionist before starting a ketogenic diet, especially for individuals with pre-existing conditions or specific dietary needs.

Why Ketogenic Diet?

The decision to follow a ketogenic diet is based on a variety of reasons, ranging from weight management and improved energy levels to specific health benefits. This approach to nutrition has gained significant popularity in recent years, partly due to the impressive results many people achieve in terms of weight loss, health markers, and overall well-being. Here are some of the main reasons people choose the ketogenic diet:

1. **Effective Weight Loss:** The ketogenic diet has proven to be an effective method for weight loss. By forcing the body to use fat instead of glucose as the main energy source, ketosis can accelerate fat loss and lead to faster weight loss. Additionally, the higher fat content in the diet can lead to a longer feeling of satiety, potentially reducing overall calorie intake.

2. **Improved Blood Sugar and Insulin Control:** For people with type 2 diabetes or prediabetes, the ketogenic diet can significantly improve blood sugar levels and better insulin sensitivity. A low carbohydrate intake prevents large blood sugar spikes, and improved fat burning can optimize the body's insulin response.

3. **Increased Energy and Mental Clarity:** After the initial adjustment phase to the ketogenic diet, many people report an increase in their energy levels and clearer mental function. Fats as an energy source can provide a more consistent energy supply compared to the fluctuations often associated with a high-carbohydrate diet.

4. **Reduction of Inflammation:** The ketogenic diet can have anti-inflammatory effects, which are due to the reduction of certain inflammatory foods and the increased intake of omega-3 fatty acids. This can help alleviate symptoms in chronic inflammatory diseases.

5. **Improvement of Heart Health:** Despite the high-fat content, the ketogenic diet, when done with healthy unsaturated fats, can have positive effects on heart health, including improvements in blood pressure, cholesterol levels, and other heart disease risk factors.

6. **Potential Therapeutic Applications:** Beyond weight loss and metabolic health, the ketogenic diet is also being researched for its potential therapeutic applications in a range of conditions, including epilepsy, Alzheimer's, and cancer. The research in these areas is ongoing, but some studies have shown promising results.

Chapter 2: Basics of the Ketogenic Diet

The second chapter of the "Ketogenic Diet Recipe Book XXL" serves to establish a solid foundation for your understanding of the ketogenic diet. Here we will delve deep into the mechanisms that make this dietary approach unique and effective. This chapter is crucial to understanding the philosophy behind the ketogenic diet and recognizing why certain foods are recommended while others should be avoided.

What is Ketosis?

Ketosis is a metabolic state in which the body uses fat as its primary energy source instead of the usual glucose from carbohydrates. This state occurs when carbohydrate availability is significantly limited, and the body is forced to shift its energy production. Here we explain in detail how ketosis works, why it is a central aspect of the ketogenic diet, and what effects it has on the body.

The Path to Ketosis

Normally, the body obtains its energy primarily by breaking down carbohydrates into glucose. With very low carbohydrate intake, as in the ketogenic diet, glucose stores in the body decrease, and it begins to search for an alternative energy source. In this process, the body turns to stored fats and converts them into so-called ketone bodies, which can then be used by cells as energy. This process occurs mainly in the liver, where fats are converted into the ketone bodies acetoacetate, β-hydroxybutyrate, and acetone.

Physiological Effects of Ketosis

- **Weight Loss:** By increasing the breakdown of fat reserves for energy production, ketosis can effectively promote weight loss.
- **Stable Energy Supply:** Ketone bodies provide a consistent energy supply, leading to fewer energy crashes compared to a carbohydrate-rich diet.
- **Reduced Hunger:** Many people report a reduced feeling of hunger in ketosis, partly due to stable blood sugar levels and the satiating effect of fats.
- **Improved Cognitive Function:** Some studies suggest that ketone bodies have a positive effect on the brain, enhancing mental clarity and concentration.

Entering and Maintaining Ketosis

To achieve ketosis, carbohydrate intake must be drastically reduced and fat intake increased. Typically, this requires limiting carbohydrate intake to less than 50 grams per day, often even less for more effective induction of ketosis. Maintaining ketosis requires continuous adherence to this macronutrient distribution, with the body becoming more efficient over time in producing and using ketone bodies.

Measuring Ketosis

The level of ketosis can be measured by various methods, in
cluding breath, blood, and urine analyses. These tests measure the amount of ketone bodies and can provide useful feedback for individuals monitoring the effectiveness of their ketogenic diet.

The Role of Macronutrients

The role of macronutrients – fats, proteins, and carbohydrates – is a central pillar of the ketogenic diet and crucial for achieving and maintaining ketosis. Each macronutrient has a specific function in the body, and the way these are balanced in the diet determines the success of the ketogenic diet. In this section, we will look in detail at the importance of each macronutrient within the ketogenic diet and explain what an optimal intake should look like.

Fats

Fats are the primary energy source in the ketogenic diet, making up the majority of daily calorie intake, typically between 70% to 80%. High fat consumption encourages the body to use fat instead of glucose as the main energy source, leading to the formation of ketone bodies.

- **Healthy Fats:** The selection of fats is crucial for health. Saturated fats (like in butter and coconut oil) are important, as well as monounsaturated and polyunsaturated fats (like in olive oil, nuts, seeds, and fatty fish). These help support the cardiovascular system and reduce inflammation in the body.

Proteins

Proteins are necessary for maintaining muscle mass, repairing tissues, and many other vital processes in the body. In the ketogenic diet, a moderate protein intake is recommended, usually between 20% to 25% of daily calorie intake. Too much protein can kick the body out of ketosis as the body can convert excess protein into glucose, a process known as gluconeogenesis.

- **High-Quality Protein Sources:** Recommended sources include meat, fish, eggs, full-fat dairy products, and plant proteins like tofu and tempeh. It is important to ensure a balanced intake to achieve optimal nutrient absorption.

Carbohydrates

Carbohydrates are severely restricted in the ketogenic diet, typically to about 5% to 10% of daily calorie intake, often less than 50 grams per day. This restriction is essential for achieving ketosis as it minimizes glucose production and forces the body to switch to fat burning.

- **Carbohydrate Sources:** The few carbohydrates consumed should mainly come from low-glycemic index vegetables, nuts, and seeds. These foods provide important nutrients and fiber alongside carbohydrates.

Macronutrient Distribution and Individual Adjustment

The specific distribution of macronutrients can vary individually, depending on factors such as age, gender, physical activity, and personal health goals. Some people may need to adjust their macronutrient distribution to achieve optimal results and effectively maintain ketosis.

Benefits of the Ketogenic Diet

The ketogenic diet offers a range of potential benefits that make it attractive to both people looking to lose weight and those aiming to improve their overall health. These benefits are based on the unique way the body metabolizes nutrients when it is in a state of ketosis. Here are some of the key benefits of the ketogenic diet, explained in detail:

Weight Loss

One of the most commonly cited motivations for choosing a ketogenic diet is weight loss. By reducing carbohydrate intake and increasing the focus on fat as an energy source, the body can burn fat more efficiently, contributing to weight reduction. Additionally, the ketogenic diet can lead to a decreased appetite since fats and proteins tend to be more satiating than carbohydrates, which reduces overall calorie intake without creating a sense of deprivation.

Improved Blood Sugar Control and Insulin Sensitivity

For people with type 2 diabetes or prediabetes, the ketogenic diet can offer significant improvement in blood sugar control. By limiting carbohydrate intake, blood sugar levels are stabilized, and the need for insulin is reduced. This not only improves glycemic control but also increases insulin sensitivity, thus reducing the risk of diabetes-related complications.

Increased Mental Clarity and Concentration

Many followers of the ketogenic diet report enhanced cognitive functions, including increased clarity and concentration. This might be partly due to ketone bodies, which provide a more efficient and stable energy source for the brain than glucose.

Reduction of Inflammation

The ketogenic diet can have anti-inflammatory effects, potentially improving a variety of inflammatory conditions. Some studies suggest that reducing carbohydrates and increasing the intake of omega-3 fatty acids, which often accompany a ketogenic diet, can contribute to a reduction in inflammation markers in the body.

Positive Effects on Heart Health

Although the ketogenic diet is high in fat, it can positively affect various risk factors for heart disease when done correctly and focusing on healthy fats. These include improvements in blood pressure, HDL cholesterol levels ("good" cholesterol), and triglyceride levels.

Potential Therapeutic Applications

Beyond the mentioned benefits, the ketogenic diet is also being explored in a broader medical context, including its potential role in the treatment or management of epilepsy, Alzheimer's disease, certain cancers, and neurological disorders. Research in these areas is ongoing, but some preliminary results are promising.

Chapter 3: Shopping List – Foods to Eat and Avoid

In this chapter of the "Ketogenic Diet Recipe Book XXL," you will receive a comprehensive guide on which foods to include in your shopping list and which to avoid to maximize the success of your ketogenic diet. Making well-considered food choices is crucial to enjoying all the benefits of the ketogenic diet while ensuring a diverse and enjoyable diet.

Foods to Eat

The foundation of the ketogenic diet consists of foods that are rich in good fats and low in carbohydrates. Here is a selection:

Fats and Oils
- Avocado oil
- Olive oil
- Coconut oil
- Butter and ghee
- Lard and tallow

Proteins
- Fatty fish varieties such as salmon, mackerel, and sardines
- Grass-fed meats including beef, lamb, and game
- Poultry, preferably dark meat for higher fat content
- Eggs
- High-quality sausages and bacon (without added sugar)

Low-Carb Vegetables
- Leafy greens like spinach, kale, and lettuce
- Cruciferous vegetables like broccoli, cauliflower, and Brussels sprouts
- Zucchini, eggplant, and bell peppers
- Mushrooms

Full-Fat Dairy Products
- Cheese
- Cream and sour cream
- Greek yogurt and cottage cheese

Nuts and Seeds
- Almonds, walnuts, macadamia nuts
- Chia seeds, flaxseeds, hemp seeds

Beverages
- Water (still and sparkling)
- Unsweetened coffee and tea
- Bone broth

Foods to Avoid

Foods that are high in sugar and starch should be avoided as they can take the body out of ketosis:

Sugar-Rich Foods
- Sweets, cakes, ice cream
- Soft drinks and sweetened beverages

Grains and Starchy Foods
- Bread, pasta, rice
- Potatoes and other starchy vegetables

Certain Dairy Products
- Milk (due to lactose content)
- Low-fat yogurts

Legumes
- Beans, lentils, peas

Processed Foods
- Fast food
- Ready meals and snacks with high sugar and trans fat content

Certain Oils and Fats
- Vegetable oils high in omega-6 fatty acids (sunflower oil, corn oil)

Alcohol
- Especially sugary alcoholic drinks like beer and sweet cocktails

BREAKFAST

1. Spinach-Feta Omelet

★★☆☆☆

🕐 10 Minutes 🍳 5 Minutes 🍴 1 servings

INSTRUCTIONS

1. Beat the eggs in a bowl and season with salt and pepper.
2. Heat olive oil in a medium-sized pan over medium heat. Add the spinach and cook briefly until just wilted.
3. Pour the beaten eggs over the spinach. Sprinkle the feta cheese and optional chopped cherry tomatoes evenly over the top.
4. Cook the omelet over medium heat until the eggs are set, occasionally lifting the edges to let the uncooked eggs flow underneath.
5. Carefully fold or flip the omelet and cook for another 1-2 minutes until fully cooked.
6. Slide onto a plate and serve immediately.

INGREDIENTS

- 3 large eggs
- 1 handful of fresh spinach, washed and roughly chopped
- 1/4 cup crumbled feta cheese
- 1 tbsp olive oil
- Salt and pepper to taste
- Optional: a few chopped cherry tomatoes for extra freshness

Nutrition Facts: Calories: 350 kcal | Protein: 22 g | Carbs: 3 g | Fat: 27 g | Fiber: 1 g | Sugar: 2 g

2. Avocado Egg Boats with Bacon

★★★☆☆

🕐 10 Minutes 🍳 15 Minutes 🍴 2 servings

INSTRUCTIONS

1. Preheat the oven to 175 degrees Celsius (350 degrees Fahrenheit).
2. Cut the avocados in half and remove the pits. Scoop out some of the flesh to create a larger cavity.
3. Place the avocado halves in a baking dish, making sure they fit snugly so they don't tip over.
4. Crack an egg into each avocado half. Season with salt and pepper.
5. Bake in the preheated oven for about 12-15 minutes, or until the eggs are cooked to your desired doneness.
6. Remove from the oven and sprinkle the crumbled bacon on top.
7. Garnish with chopped fresh chives and serve warm.

INGREDIENTS

- 2 ripe avocados
- 4 small eggs
- 2 slices of bacon, cooked and crumbled
- Salt and pepper to taste
- Chopped fresh chives for garnish

Nutrition Facts : Calories: 320 kcal | Protein: 12 g | Carbs: 8 g | Fat: 28 g | Fiber: 6 g | Sugar: 1 g

3. Keto Frittata with Mushrooms, Zucchini, and Cheese

★★☆☆☆

10 Minutes | 20 Minutes | 4 servings

INGREDIENTS
- 8 large eggs
- 1/2 cup heavy cream
- 1 cup mushrooms, sliced
- 1 medium zucchini, diced
- 1 cup shredded cheese (cheddar, mozzarella, or your preferred type)
- 2 tablespoons olive oil
- 2 cloves garlic, minced
- Salt and pepper to taste
- Fresh parsley, chopped (optional for garnish)

INSTRUCTIONS
1. Preheat your oven to 175 degrees Celsius (350 degrees Fahrenheit).
2. In a large bowl, whisk together the eggs and heavy cream until well combined. Season with salt and pepper.
3. Heat the olive oil in an oven-safe skillet over medium heat. Add the minced garlic and sauté until fragrant, about 1 minute.
4. Add the sliced mushrooms and diced zucchini to the skillet. Cook until the vegetables are tender and any moisture has evaporated, about 5-7 minutes.
5. Spread the vegetables evenly in the skillet and pour the egg mixture over them. Tilt the skillet to ensure the eggs cover the vegetables evenly.
6. Sprinkle the shredded cheese evenly over the top of the egg mixture.
7. Transfer the skillet to the preheated oven and bake for 15-20 minutes, or until the frittata is set and the top is golden brown.
8. Remove from the oven and let it cool slightly before slicing. Garnish with chopped fresh parsley if desired.
9. Serve warm and enjoy.

Nutrition Facts: Calories: 280 kcal | Protein: 15 g | Carbs: 4 g | Fat: 23 g | Fiber: 1 g | Sugar: 2 g

4. Keto Baked Pumpkin Slices with Herbs and Garlic

★★★☆☆

10 Minutes | 25 Minutes | 4 servings

INGREDIENTS
- 500 g pumpkin, peeled and sliced into thin wedges
- 2 tablespoons olive oil
- 3 cloves garlic, minced
- 1 teaspoon dried rosemary
- 1 teaspoon dried thyme
- Salt and pepper to taste
- Fresh parsley, chopped (optional for garnish)

INSTRUCTIONS
1. Preheat your oven to 200 degrees Celsius (400 degrees Fahrenheit).
2. In a large bowl, toss the pumpkin slices with olive oil, minced garlic, dried rosemary, dried thyme, salt, and pepper until well coated.
3. Arrange the pumpkin slices in a single layer on a baking sheet lined with parchment paper.
4. Bake in the preheated oven for 20-25 minutes, or until the pumpkin is tender and slightly caramelized around the edges.
5. Remove from the oven and let cool slightly before serving. Garnish with chopped fresh parsley if desired.
6. Serve warm and enjoy as a healthy snack or side dish.

Nutrition Facts: Calories: 80 kcal | Protein: 1 g | Carbs: 7 g | Fat: 6 g | Fiber: 2 g | Sugar: 3 g

5. Keto Toast with Salmon, Avocado, Poached Egg, and Cheese

★★★★☆

5 Minutes | 0 Minutes | 2 servings

INSTRUCTIONS

1. Toast the Bread: Lightly toast the slice of keto-friendly bread.
2. Prepare the Avocado: Mash the avocado in a small bowl and season with a pinch of salt and pepper.
3. Poach the Egg: Bring a small pot of water to a simmer. Crack the egg into a small bowl or cup. Create a gentle whirlpool in the pot with a spoon and gently slide the egg into the center. Poach for 3-4 minutes until the white is set but the yolk is still runny. Remove with a slotted spoon and drain on a paper towel.
4. Assemble the Toast: Spread the cream cheese on the toasted bread. Top with the mashed avocado, then lay the smoked salmon on top.
5. Add the Poached Egg: Carefully place the poached egg on top of the salmon.
6. Season and Garnish: Season with salt and pepper. Garnish with fresh dill or chives if desired.
7. Serve: Serve immediately and enjoy!

INGREDIENTS

- 1 slice keto-friendly bread (such as almond flour or coconut flour bread)
- 1/4 avocado, mashed
- 1 slice smoked salmon
- 1 poached egg
- 1 tablespoon cream cheese or a slice of your favorite cheese
- Salt and pepper to taste
- Fresh dill or chives for garnish (optional)

Nutrition Facts : Calories: 350 kcal | Protein: 18 g | Carbs: 5 g | Fat: 28 g | Fiber: 4 g | Sugar: 1 g

6. Fried Eggs with Broccoli and Cheese

★★★☆☆

5 Minutes | 10 Minutes | 2 servings

INSTRUCTIONS

1. Prepare Broccoli: In a medium skillet, heat 1 tablespoon of olive oil or butter over medium heat. Add the chopped broccoli florets and sauté for 3-4 minutes, until they start to become tender.
2. Cook Eggs: Push the broccoli to the side of the skillet and add the remaining tablespoon of olive oil or butter. Crack the eggs into the skillet, season with salt and pepper, and cook until the whites are set but the yolks are still runny, or to your desired level of doneness.
3. Add Cheese: Sprinkle the shredded cheddar cheese over the eggs and broccoli. Cover the skillet with a lid and cook for another 1-2 minutes, until the cheese is melted.
4. Serve: Plate the eggs and broccoli, making sure to get a good mix of both in each serving. Enjoy hot.

INGREDIENTS

- 4 large eggs
- 1 cup broccoli florets, chopped
- 1/2 cup shredded cheddar cheese
- 2 tablespoons olive oil or butter
- Salt and pepper to taste

Nutrition Facts : Calories: 300 kcal | Protein: 18 g | Carbs: 4 g | Fat: 24 g | Fiber: 2 g | Sugar: 1 g

7. Keto Toasts with Ricotta, Egg, Cucumber, and Black Sesame

★★★☆☆

10 Minutes | 5 Minutes | 2 servings

INGREDIENTS

- 2 slices of keto-friendly bread
- 1/2 cup ricotta cheese
- 2 large eggs
- 1/2 cucumber, thinly sliced
- 1 tsp black sesame seeds
- Salt and pepper to taste
- Fresh herbs (optional, e.g., dill or parsley)

INSTRUCTIONS

1. Prepare the Eggs: Boil or fry the eggs to your preferred doneness (boiled, poached, or fried).
2. Toast the Bread: Lightly toast the keto-friendly bread slices until golden brown.
3. Assemble the Toasts: Spread ricotta cheese evenly on each toast. Top with slices of cucumber and the cooked eggs.
4. Season and Garnish: Sprinkle black sesame seeds, salt, and pepper over the toasts. Garnish with fresh herbs if desired.
5. Serve: Serve immediately while the toasts are still warm.

Nutrition Facts : Calories: 250 kcal | Protein: 14 g | Carbs: 6 g | Fat: 18 g | Fiber: 3 g | Sugar: 2 g

8. Asparagus with Prosciutto, Avocado, and Fried Eggs

★★★☆☆

10 Minutes | 15 Minutes | 2 servings

INGREDIENTS

- 1 bunch asparagus, trimmed
- 4 slices prosciutto
- 1 ripe avocado, sliced
- 4 large eggs
- 2 tbsp olive oil (or butter)
- Salt and pepper to taste
- Fresh herbs (optional, for garnish)

INSTRUCTIONS

1. Prepare the Asparagus: Heat 1 tbsp of olive oil (or butter) in a large skillet over medium heat. Add the asparagus and sauté until tender, about 5-7 minutes. Season with salt and pepper.
2. Cook the Prosciutto: In the same skillet, crisp up the prosciutto slices for about 1-2 minutes on each side. Remove and set aside.
3. Fry the Eggs: In the same skillet, add another 1 tbsp of olive oil (or butter). Crack the eggs into the skillet and cook to your desired doneness (sunny-side up, over-easy, etc.). Season with salt and pepper.
4. Assemble the Plate: Arrange the sautéed asparagus on two plates.
5. Add the crispy prosciutto and sliced avocado on top. Place the fried eggs on the side or on top of the asparagus and prosciutto.
6. Garnish and Serve: Garnish with fresh herbs if desired and serve immediately.

Nutrition Facts : Calories: 400 kcal | Protein: 18 g | Carbs: 8 g | Fat: 32 g | Fiber: 7 g | Sugar: 2 g

9. Fried Eggs with Vegetables

★★★☆☆

10 Minutes | 15 Minutes | 2 servings

INGREDIENTS

- 4 large eggs
- 1 cup broccoli florets
- 1 bell pepper, sliced
- 1 zucchini, sliced
- 1/2 cup cherry tomatoes, halved
- 2 tbsp olive oil (or butter)
- Salt and pepper to taste
- Fresh herbs (optional, for garnish)

INSTRUCTIONS

1. Prepare the Vegetables: Heat 1 tbsp of olive oil (or butter) in a large skillet over medium heat. Add the broccoli, bell pepper, and zucchini. Sauté for about 5-7 minutes, until the vegetables are tender but still crisp. Add the cherry tomatoes and cook for another 2 minutes. Season with salt and pepper.
2. Cook the Eggs: In a separate skillet, heat the remaining 1 tbsp of olive oil (or butter) over medium heat. Crack the eggs into the skillet and cook until the whites are set and the yolks reach your desired doneness (sunny-side up, over-easy, etc.). Season with salt and pepper.
3. Assemble the Plate: Divide the sautéed vegetables between two plates. Place the fried eggs on top of the vegetables.
4. Garnish and Serve: Garnish with fresh herbs if desired and serve immediately.

Nutrition Facts: Calories: 300 kcal | Protein: 14 g | Carbs: 10 g | Fat: 24 g | Fiber: 4 g | Sugar: 5 g

10. Keto Yogurt with Chocolate Pieces and Crumbs

★★★☆☆

10 Minutes | 0 Minutes | 4 servings

INGREDIENTS

- 2 cups heavy cream or full-fat Greek yogurt (ensure it is unsweetened and has no added sugar)
- 1/4 cup sugar-free dark chocolate, chopped into small pieces
- 1/4 cup keto-friendly chocolate crumbs (made from almond flour, cocoa powder, and a keto-friendly sweetener like erythritol)
- 1 tsp vanilla extract
- Optional: A few drops of liquid stevia or other keto-friendly sweeteners if additional sweetness is desired

INSTRUCTIONS

1. Prepare the Chocolate Crumbs: Mix 1/4 cup almond flour, 1 tbsp unsweetened cocoa powder, and 2 tbsp erythritol in a bowl. Spread the mixture on a baking sheet and toast in a preheated oven at 150°C (300°F) for about 10 minutes, stirring halfway through. Let cool and crumble.
2. Mix the Yogurt: In a bowl, combine the heavy cream or full-fat Greek yogurt with the vanilla extract and optional sweetener. Mix well.
3. Add the Chocolate: Fold in the chopped sugar-free dark chocolate pieces and the cooled chocolate crumbs.
4. Serve: Divide the mixture into four servings and serve immediately, or refrigerate for later use.

Nutrition Facts: Calories: 300 kcal | Protein: 4 g | Carbs: 5 g | Fat: 30 g | Fiber: 2 g | Sugar: 2 g

11. Low-Carb Blueberry Smoothie

★★★★★

10 Minutes | 15 Minutes | 2 servings

INGREDIENTS

- 1 cup unsweetened almond milk
- 1/2 cup fresh or frozen blueberries
- 1/2 avocado
- 1 tbsp chia seeds
- 1 tbsp MCT oil or coconut oil
- 1 tsp vanilla extract

INSTRUCTIONS

1. Combine all ingredients in a blender.
2. Blend until smooth.
3. Pour into glasses and serve immediately.

Nutrition Facts : Calories: 180 kcal | Protein: 3 g | Carbs: 8 g | Fat: 15 g | Fiber: 6 g | Sugar: 3 g

---

12. Keto Berry Fruit Smoothie

★★★★★

15 Minutes | 15 Minutes | 2 servings

INGREDIENTS

- 1/2 cup unsweetened almond milk
- 1/2 cup full-fat coconut milk
- 1/2 cup frozen mixed berries (raspberries, blackberries, strawberries)
- 1/4 avocado
- 1 tablespoon chia seeds
- 1 tablespoon almond butter
- 1/2 teaspoon vanilla extract
- A few drops of liquid stevia or another keto-friendly sweetener, to taste
- Ice cubes (optional)

INSTRUCTIONS

1. Combine Ingredients: In a blender, combine the unsweetened almond milk, full-fat coconut milk, frozen mixed berries, avocado, chia seeds, almond butter, and vanilla extract.
2. Blend: Blend until smooth and creamy. If the smoothie is too thick, add a bit more almond milk to reach your desired consistency.
3. Sweeten: Taste the smoothie and add liquid stevia or another keto-friendly sweetener if needed. Blend again to mix well.
4. Serve: Pour the smoothie into glasses. Add ice cubes if desired for a colder drink.

Nutrition Facts : Calories: 210 kcal | Protein: 4 g | Carbs: 10 g (Net Carbs: 5 g) | Fat: 18 g | Fiber: 5 g |

12. Green Smoothie with Spinach and Fresh Green Vegetables

★★★☆☆

🕐 10 Minutes | 🍳 0 Minutes | 🍴 2 servings

INGREDIENTS

- 2 cups fresh spinach leaves
- 1/2 avocado
- 1/2 cucumber
- 1 celery stalk
- 1/4 cup fresh parsley
- 1/4 cup fresh mint leaves
- 1 tbsp chia seeds
- 1 cup unsweetened almond milk
- 1 tbsp lemon juice
- Ice cubes (optional)

INSTRUCTIONS

1. Prepare the Vegetables: Wash and roughly chop the spinach, avocado, cucumber, celery, parsley, and mint leaves.
2. Blend the Ingredients: In a blender, combine all the prepared vegetables, chia seeds, almond milk, lemon juice, and ice cubes (if using).
3. Blend until smooth and creamy. If the smoothie is too thick, add more almond milk to reach the desired consistency.
4. Serve: Pour the smoothie into glasses and serve immediately.

Nutrition Facts : Calories: 120 kcal | Protein: 3 g | Carbs: 7 g | Fat: 9 g | Fiber: 5 g | Sugar: 1 g

14. Avocado Keto Chocolate Pudding

★★★☆☆

🕐 10 Minutes | 🍳 0 Minutes | 🍴 2 servings

INGREDIENTS

- 2 ripe avocados, pitted and peeled
- 1/4 cup unsweetened cocoa powder
- 1/4 cup erythritol (or other keto-friendly sweetener)
- 1/2 cup coconut milk
- 1 tsp vanilla extract

INSTRUCTIONS

1. Combine all ingredients in a high-powered blender.
2. Blend until smooth and creamy.
3. Divide into bowls and chill for at least one hour before serving.

Nutrition Facts : Calories: 345 kcal | Protein: 4 g | Carbs: 15 g | Fat: 31 g | Fiber: 10 g | Sugar: 1 g

GRAINS, LEGUME

15. Zucchini Hummus

★★★★★

10 Minutes | 0 Minutes | 4 servings

INGREDIENTS

- 2 medium zucchinis, chopped
- 1/4 cup tahini
- 2 tbsp olive oil
- 1 garlic clove, minced
- Juice of 1 lemon
- Salt and pepper to taste
- Paprika for garnish

INSTRUCTIONS

1. Combine all ingredients except paprika in a blender or food processor and blend until smooth.
2. Transfer to a serving bowl and garnish with paprika.
3. Serve with keto-friendly crackers or vegetables.

Nutrition Facts : Calories: 150 kcal | Protein: 4 g | Carbs: 6 g | Fat: 12 g | Fiber: 2 g | Sugar: 3 g

16. Keto Lentil Soup with Vegetables

★★★★★

15 Minutes | 30 Minutes | 4 servings

INGREDIENTS

- 1 large head of cauliflower, finely chopped
- 1 tbsp olive oil
- 1 onion, diced
- 2 carrots, chopped
- 2 celery stalks, chopped
- 2 garlic cloves, minced
- 1 can (400 g) diced tomatoes
- 4 cups vegetable broth
- 1 tsp dried thyme
- Salt and pepper to taste
- Fresh parsley for garnish

INSTRUCTIONS

1. Heat olive oil in a large pot over medium heat. Add the onion, carrots, celery, and garlic, and sauté until softened.
2. Add the chopped cauliflower, diced tomatoes, vegetable broth, and thyme. Bring to a boil, then reduce heat and simmer for 20-25 minutes.
3. Season with salt and pepper, and garnish with fresh parsley before serving.

Nutrition Facts : Calories: 180 kcal | Protein: 5 g | Carbs: 14 g | Fat: 9 g | Fiber: 6 g | Sugar: 8 g

17. Avocado Green Bean Purée (Peas from Green Beans)

★★★☆☆

⏱ 10 Minutes | 🍳 10 Minutes | 🍴 2 servings

INGREDIENTS

- 1 cup green beans, chopped
- 1 ripe avocado
- 1 garlic clove, minced
- Juice of 1 lime
- Salt and pepper to taste

INSTRUCTIONS

1. Cook green beans in boiling water for 5-7 minutes until tender. Drain and let cool.
2. In a blender or food processor, combine green beans, avocado, garlic, lime juice, salt, and pepper. Blend until smooth.
3. Serve as a side dish or dip.

Nutrition Facts: Calories: 200 kcal | Protein: 4 g | Carbs: 10 g | Fat: 18 g | Fiber: 7 g | Sugar: 2 g

18. Keto-Friendly Broccoli with Cheese Cream

★★★★☆

⏱ 10 Minutes | 🍳 15 Minutes | 🍴 2 servings

INGREDIENTS

- 500 g broccoli florets
- 1 cup heavy cream
- 1 cup shredded cheddar cheese
- 2 tablespoons cream cheese
- 1 garlic clove, minced
- Salt and pepper to taste
- 1 tablespoon olive oil

INSTRUCTIONS

1. Prepare Broccoli: In a large pot, bring water to a boil. Add the broccoli florets and cook for 5-7 minutes until tender. Drain and set aside.
2. Make Cheese Cream: In a saucepan over medium heat, add the olive oil and minced garlic. Sauté until fragrant, about 1 minute. Add the heavy cream and bring to a gentle simmer. Stir in the shredded cheddar cheese and cream cheese until melted and well combined. Season with salt and pepper to taste.
3. Combine and Serve: Add the cooked broccoli to the saucepan with the cheese cream. Toss to coat the broccoli evenly with the cheese sauce. Serve hot in a bowl.

Nutrition Facts: Calories: 340 kcal | Protein: 12 g | Carbs: 8 g (Net Carbs: 5 g) | Fat: 30 g | Fiber: 3 g |

19. Keto Sauerkraut Salad with Cranberries and Black Pepper

★★★☆☆

10 Minutes | 0 Minutes | 2 servings

INGREDIENTS

- 2 cups sauerkraut (drained)
- 1/4 cup dried cranberries (sugar-free)
- 1 tablespoon black peppercorns, crushed
- 2 tablespoons olive oil
- 1 tablespoon apple cider vinegar
- Fresh parsley for garnish

INSTRUCTIONS

1. Prepare Ingredients: Drain the sauerkraut and place it in a large bowl. Crush the black peppercorns using a mortar and pestle or a rolling pin.
2. Combine Ingredients: Add the dried cranberries and crushed black peppercorns to the bowl with sauerkraut. Drizzle the olive oil and apple cider vinegar over the mixture.
3. Mix and Garnish: Toss all the ingredients together until well combined. Garnish with fresh parsley.
4. Serve: Serve immediately or refrigerate for an hour to let the flavors meld together.

Nutrition Facts: Calories: 120 kcal | Protein: 2 g | Carbs: 10 g (Net Carbs: 6 g) | Fat: 8 g | Fiber: 4 g |

20. Zucchini Noodles with Flavorful Marinara Sauce and Vegan Parmesan

★★★★☆

10 Minutes | 20 Minutes | 4 servings

INGREDIENTS

- 4 large zucchinis, spiralized
- 1 tablespoon olive oil
- 2 cups marinara sauce
- 1/4 cup vegan parmesan cheese, grated
- Salt and pepper to taste
- Fresh basil, for garnish

INSTRUCTIONS

1. Heat olive oil in a large skillet over medium heat. Add spiralized zucchini noodles and sauté for 3-5 minutes, just until tender.
2. Add marinara sauce to the skillet, stirring to coat the noodles. Cook for an additional 5 minutes, allowing the flavors to meld.
3. Season with salt and pepper.
4. Serve hot, sprinkled with vegan parmesan and garnished with fresh basil.

NuNutritional: Calories: 160 kcal | Protein: 4 g | Carbohydrates: 18 g | Fat: 8 g | Fiber: 4 g | Sugar: 10 g

21. Cucumber Salad with Tomatoes and Feta Cheese

★★★★★

10 Minutes | 0 Minutes | 4 servings

INGREDIENTS

- 2 large cucumbers, diced
- 1 cup cherry tomatoes, halved
- 1/2 cup feta cheese, crumbled
- 1/4 cup red onion, thinly sliced
- 2 tablespoons olive oil
- 1 tablespoon red wine vinegar
- Salt and pepper to taste
- Fresh dill, chopped, for garnish

INSTRUCTIONS

1. In a large bowl, combine cucumbers, cherry tomatoes, feta cheese, and red onion.
2. Drizzle with olive oil and red wine vinegar, then toss to combine.
3. Season with salt and pepper.
4. Garnish with chopped dill before serving.
5. Serve chilled for a refreshing side dish.

Nutritional: Calories: 160 kcal | Protein: 4 g | Carbohydrates: 10 g | Fat: 12 g | Fiber: 2 g | Sugar: 5 g

22. Salad with Asparagus, Feta Cheese, Pine Nuts, and Lemon

★★★★★

15 Minutes | 10 Minutes | 4 servings

INGREDIENTS

- 1 pound asparagus, trimmed and cut into 1-inch pieces
- 1/2 cup pine nuts, toasted
- 1/2 cup feta cheese, crumbled
- Zest and juice of 1 lemon
- 1/4 cup olive oil
- Salt and pepper to taste

INSTRUCTIONS

1. Bring a pot of salted water to a boil. Add asparagus and cook for 3 minutes until bright green and slightly tender. Drain and plunge into ice water to stop cooking.
2. In a large bowl, combine blanched asparagus, toasted pine nuts, and crumbled feta cheese.
3. In a small bowl, whisk together lemon zest, lemon juice, and olive oil. Season with salt and pepper.
4. Pour the dressing over the salad and toss gently to combine.
5. Serve immediately or chill in the refrigerator before serving.

Nutritional: Calories: 300 kcal | Protein: 8 g | Carbohydrates: 10 g | Fat: 27 g | Fiber: 3 g | Sugar: 4 g

SIDES AND VEGETABLE

23. Asparagus with Poached Egg and Jamon Serrano

★★★☆☆

🕐 10 Minutes   🍳 10 Minutes   🍴 2 servings

INGREDIENTS

- 1 bunch of asparagus (about 12 spears)
- 2 large eggs
- 4 slices of Jamon Serrano (or prosciutto)
- 1 tbsp white vinegar
- 1 tbsp olive oil
- Salt and pepper to taste
- Optional: grated Parmesan for serving

INSTRUCTIONS

1. Prepare Asparagus: Trim the tough ends off the asparagus. Heat olive oil in a large pan over medium heat. Add the asparagus and sauté for 5-7 minutes until tender-crisp. Season with salt and pepper. Transfer to serving plates.
2. Poach Eggs: Fill a saucepan with water and bring to a gentle simmer. Add vinegar. Crack each egg into a small bowl, then gently slide the eggs into the water. Poach for 3-4 minutes until the whites are set but the yolks are still runny. Remove with a slotted spoon and drain on a paper towel.
3. Assemble: Lay the slices of Jamon Serrano over the asparagus.
4. Top with Egg: Place a poached egg on top of each plate.
5. Serve: Sprinkle with grated Parmesan if desired, and season with a little more salt and pepper. Serve immediately.

Nutrition : Calories: 210 kcal | Protein: 15 g | Carbs: 4 g | Fat: 15 g | Fiber: 2 g | Sugar: 2 g

24. Salad of Greens, Avocado, and Cucumbers

★★☆☆☆

🕐 15 Minutes   🍳 10 Minutes   🍴 4 servings

INGREDIENTS

- 4 cups mixed salad greens (e.g., lettuce, spinach, arugula)
- 1 ripe avocado, diced
- 1 cucumber, thinly sliced
- 1/4 red onion, thinly sliced
- 2 tbsp olive oil
- 1 tbsp lemon juice
- Salt and pepper to taste
- Fresh dill or parsley for garnish (optional)

INSTRUCTIONS

1. Prepare Salad: In a large bowl, combine mixed salad greens, diced avocado, thinly sliced cucumber, and red onion.
2. Make Dressing: In a small bowl, whisk together olive oil, lemon juice, salt, and pepper.
3. Combine: Drizzle the dressing over the salad and toss gently to combine.
4. Serve: Garnish with fresh dill or parsley if desired. Serve immediately.

Nutrition Facts: Calories: 210 kcal | Protein: 3 g | Carbs: 10 g | Fat: 19 g | Fiber: 7 g | Sugar: 2 g

25. Avocado, Tomatoes, Eggs, and Lettuce Salad

★★★☆☆

⏱ 10 Minutes   🔥 10 Minutes   🍴 2 servings

INGREDIENTS

- 1 ripe avocado, sliced
- 2 hard-boiled eggs, quartered
- 1 cup cherry tomatoes, halved
- 2 cups mixed lettuce leaves
- 2 tbsp olive oil
- 1 tbsp lemon juice
- Salt and pepper to taste

INSTRUCTIONS

1. Prepare Ingredients: Arrange the mixed lettuce leaves on a large plate.
2. Add Vegetables and Eggs: Top with sliced avocado, quartered hard-boiled eggs, and halved cherry tomatoes.
3. Make Dressing: In a small bowl, whisk together olive oil, lemon juice, salt, and pepper.
4. Combine: Drizzle the dressing over the salad and gently toss to combine.
5. Serve: Serve immediately.

Nutrition : Calories: 210 kcal | Protein: 15 g | Carbs: 4 g | Fat: 15 g | Fiber: 2 g | Sugar: 2 g

26. Simple Salad with Tomatoes, Cucumber, Red Onions, and Lettuce

★★★☆☆

⏱ 10 Minutes   🔥 0 Minutes   🍴 2 servings

INGREDIENTS

- 2 cups lettuce leaves, chopped
- 1 cup cherry tomatoes, halved
- 1 cucumber, sliced
- 1/4 red onion, thinly sliced
- 2 tbsp olive oil
- 1 tbsp lemon juice
- Salt and pepper to taste
- Fresh herbs (e.g., parsley, basil) for garnish

INSTRUCTIONS

1. Prepare Vegetables: Wash and chop the lettuce leaves. Halve the cherry tomatoes, slice the cucumber, and thinly slice the red onion.
2. Combine Ingredients: In a large bowl, combine lettuce, cherry tomatoes, cucumber, and red onion.
3. Make Dressing: In a small bowl, whisk together olive oil, lemon juice, salt, and pepper.
4. Toss Salad: Pour the dressing over the salad and toss gently to combine.
5. Garnish and Serve: Garnish with fresh herbs if desired. Serve immediately.

Nutrition Facts: Calories: 210 kcal | Protein: 3 g | Carbs: 10 g | Fat: 19 g | Fiber: 7 g | Sugar: 2 g

27. Caprese Salad with Cherry Tomatoes, Mozzarella, and Basil

★★☆☆☆

10 Minutes | 0 Minutes | 2 servings

INGREDIENTS

- 2 cups cherry tomatoes, halved
- 1 cup mozzarella balls (bocconcini)
- 1/4 cup fresh basil leaves
- 2 tbsp olive oil
- 1 tbsp balsamic vinegar
- Salt and pepper to taste

INSTRUCTIONS

1. Prepare Ingredients: Halve the cherry tomatoes and drain the mozzarella balls.
2. Assemble Salad: In a serving bowl, combine the cherry tomatoes, mozzarella balls, and fresh basil leaves.
3. Add Dressing: Drizzle olive oil and balsamic vinegar over the salad. Season with salt and pepper to taste.
4. Toss and Serve: Gently toss the salad to mix the ingredients and serve immediately.

Nutrition Facts: Calories: 200 kcal | Protein: 10 g | Carbs: 6 g | Fat: 16 g | Fiber: 2 g | Sugar: 4 g

28. Grilled Vegetables

★★★☆☆

10 Minutes | 0 Minutes | 2 servings

INGREDIENTS

- 2 bell peppers, sliced
- 2 zucchinis, sliced
- 1 cup mushrooms, sliced
- 1 cup cherry tomatoes, halved
- 2 tbsp olive oil
- 1 tsp garlic powder
- 1 tsp dried oregano
- Salt and pepper to taste

INSTRUCTIONS

1. Preheat Grill: Preheat your grill or grill pan to medium-high heat.
2. Prepare Vegetables: In a large bowl, combine bell peppers, zucchinis, mushrooms, and cherry tomatoes.
3. Season: Drizzle the vegetables with olive oil and sprinkle with garlic powder, dried oregano, salt, and pepper. Toss to coat evenly.
4. Grill: Place the vegetables on the grill or grill pan in a single layer. Grill for 15-20 minutes, turning occasionally, until the vegetables are tender and have grill marks.
5. Serve: Remove from the grill and serve hot.

Nutrition Facts: Calories: 90 kcal | Protein: 2 g | Carbs: 7 g | Fat: 7 g | Fiber: 2 g | Sugar: 4 g

29. Broccoli Salad with Cherry Tomatoes and Almonds

★★☆☆

15 Minutes 0 Minutes 4 servings

INGREDIENTS

- 4 cups broccoli florets
- 1 cup cherry tomatoes, halved
- 1/2 cup sliced almonds
- 1/4 cup red onion, thinly sliced
- 2 tbsp olive oil
- 1 tbsp apple cider vinegar
- 1 tsp Dijon mustard
- Salt and pepper to taste

INSTRUCTIONS

1. Prepare Vegetables: In a large bowl, combine broccoli florets, halved cherry tomatoes, sliced almonds, and red onion.
2. Make Dressing: In a small bowl, whisk together olive oil, apple cider vinegar, Dijon mustard, salt, and pepper until well combined.
3. Toss Salad: Pour the dressing over the broccoli mixture and toss until all the ingredients are evenly coated.
4. Chill: Let the salad sit in the refrigerator for at least 15 minutes before serving to allow the flavors to meld together.
5. Serve: Serve chilled or at room temperature.

Nutrition Facts: Calories: 160 kcal | Protein: 4 g | Carbs: 9 g | Fat: 13 g | Fiber: 4 g | Sugar: 3 g

30. Grilled Vegetables with Herbs

★★★☆☆

10 Minutes 15 Minutes 4 servings

INGREDIENTS

- 2 bell peppers, sliced
- 1 zucchini, sliced
- 1 eggplant, sliced
- 1 red onion, sliced
- 200 g mushrooms, halved
- 3 tbsp olive oil
- 2 tsp dried Italian herbs (oregano, basil, thyme)
- Salt and pepper to taste
- Fresh parsley, chopped (for garnish)

INSTRUCTIONS

1. Prepare Vegetables: In a large bowl, combine bell peppers, zucchini, eggplant, red onion, and mushrooms.
2. Season: Drizzle olive oil over the vegetables and sprinkle with dried Italian herbs, salt, and pepper. Toss to coat evenly.
3. Grill: Preheat a grill or grill pan over medium-high heat. Place the vegetables on the grill and cook for about 5-7 minutes on each side, or until tender and slightly charred.
4. Serve: Transfer the grilled vegetables to a serving platter and garnish with fresh parsley.

Nutrition Facts: Calories: 110 kcal | Protein: 2 g | Carbs: 8 g | Fat: 8 g | Fiber: 3 g | Sugar: 5 g

31. Grilled Avocado Salad with Greens

★★☆☆☆

🕐 10 Minutes | 🥄🕐 0 Minutes | 🍴 2 servings

INGREDIENTS

- 2 ripe avocados, halved and pitted
- 4 cups mixed green leaves (spinach, arugula, kale)
- 1/4 cup red onion, thinly sliced
- 1/4 cup cherry tomatoes, halved
- 2 tbsp olive oil
- 1 tbsp lemon juice
- Salt and pepper to taste
- Fresh herbs (parsley, cilantro) for garnish

INSTRUCTIONS

1. Grill Avocado: Preheat a grill or grill pan over medium heat. Brush the avocado halves with 1 tbsp of olive oil. Place the avocado halves on the grill, cut side down, and grill for 2-3 minutes until grill marks appear. Remove and let cool slightly.
2. Prepare Salad: In a large bowl, combine mixed green leaves, red onion, and cherry tomatoes.
3. Make Dressing: In a small bowl, whisk together the remaining olive oil, lemon juice, salt, and pepper.
4. Assemble Salad: Scoop out the grilled avocado and slice it. Add the avocado slices to the salad. Drizzle with the dressing and toss gently to combine.
5. Serve: Garnish with fresh herbs and serve immediately.

Nutrition Facts: Calories: 240 kcal | Protein: 3 g | Carbs: 14 g | Fat: 22 g | Fiber: 10 g | Sugar: 3 g

32. Roasted Brussels Sprouts with Bacon

★★★☆☆

🕐 10 Minutes | 🥄🕐 25 Minutes | 🍴 4 servings

INGREDIENTS

- 500 g Brussels sprouts, trimmed and halved
- 6 slices bacon, chopped
- 2 tbsp olive oil
- Salt and pepper to taste
- Optional: 1 tbsp balsamic vinegar

INSTRUCTIONS

1. Preheat the Oven: Preheat your oven to 200°C (400°F).
2. Prepare the Brussels Sprouts: In a large bowl, toss the Brussels sprouts with olive oil, salt, and pepper.
3. Combine with Bacon: Add the chopped bacon to the Brussels sprouts and mix well.
4. Roast: Spread the Brussels sprouts and bacon mixture in a single layer on a baking sheet. Roast in the preheated oven for 20-25 minutes, stirring halfway through, until the Brussels sprouts are tender and caramelized and the bacon is crispy.
5. Optional Glaze: If desired, drizzle with balsamic vinegar before serving.

Nutrition Facts: Calories: 200 kcal | Protein: 7 g | Carbs: 10 g | Fat: 15 g | Fiber: 4 g | Sugar: 2 g

33. Green Vegetable and Avocado Salad

★★☆☆☆

🕐 15 Minutes   🍳 0 Minutes   🍴 2 servings

INGREDIENTS

- 2 cups mixed salad lettuce
- 1 cucumber, sliced
- 1 leek, thinly sliced
- 1 avocado, diced
- 1 green bell pepper, diced
- 1 tbsp olive oil
- Juice of 1 lemon
- Salt and pepper to taste

INSTRUCTIONS

1. Prepare the Salad: In a large bowl, combine the salad lettuce, cucumber, leek, avocado, and green bell pepper.
2. Make the Dressing: In a small bowl, whisk together the olive oil, lemon juice, salt, and pepper.
3. Assemble the Salad: Drizzle the dressing over the salad and toss gently to combine.
4. Serve: Serve immediately as a refreshing keto-friendly side dish or a light meal.

Nutrition Facts: Calories: 180 kcal | Protein: 3 g | Carbs: 10 g | Fat: 15 g | Fiber: 7 g | Sugar: 3 g

34. Keto Eggplant with Low-Carb Sweet Glaze

★★★☆☆

🕐 15 Minutes   🍳 20 Minutes   🍴 4 servings

INGREDIENTS

- 2 large eggplants, sliced into rounds
- 2 tbsp olive oil
- 1 tbsp low-carb sweetener (such as erythritol or stevia)
- 2 tbsp soy sauce
- 1 tbsp apple cider vinegar
- 2 cloves garlic, minced
- Salt and pepper to taste
- Fresh parsley for garnish

INSTRUCTIONS

1. Preheat Oven: Preheat your oven to 200°C (400°F).
2. Prepare Eggplant: Arrange the eggplant slices on a baking sheet and brush both sides with olive oil. Season with salt and pepper.
3. Bake Eggplant: Bake in the preheated oven for 15-20 minutes, flipping halfway through, until the eggplant is tender and golden brown.
4. Prepare Glaze: While the eggplant is baking, combine the low-carb sweetener, soy sauce, apple cider vinegar, and minced garlic in a small bowl. Stir well to combine.
5. Glaze Eggplant: Once the eggplant is done baking, remove from the oven and brush the sweet glaze over the eggplant slices.
6. Serve: Garnish with fresh parsley and serve warm.

Nutrition Facts : Calories: 90 kcal | Protein: 2 g | Carbs: 6 g | Fat: 7 g | Fiber: 3 g | Sugar: 2 g

35. Fried Mushrooms and Broccoli

★★☆☆☆

10 Minutes | 15 Minutes | 2 servings

INGREDIENTS

- 200g broccoli florets
- 200g mushrooms, sliced
- 2 tbsp olive oil
- 2 garlic cloves, minced
- Salt and pepper to taste
- 1 tbsp soy sauce (optional)
- 1 tsp sesame seeds (optional)

INSTRUCTIONS

1. Prepare the Vegetables: Wash and cut the broccoli into florets and slice the mushrooms.
2. Heat the Olive Oil: In a large skillet, heat the olive oil over medium heat.
3. Cook the Garlic: Add the minced garlic to the skillet and sauté for about 1 minute until fragrant.
4. Add the Vegetables: Add the broccoli and mushrooms to the skillet. Cook for about 10-12 minutes, stirring occasionally, until the vegetables are tender.
5. Season: Season with salt and pepper to taste. If using, add soy sauce and stir to combine.
6. Serve: Transfer the fried mushrooms and broccoli to a serving plate. Sprinkle with sesame seeds if desired and serve immediately.

Nutrition Facts: Calories: 120 kcal | Protein: 4 g | Carbs: 10 g | Fat: 8 g | Fiber: 4 g | Sugar: 2 g

36. Zucchini Noodles with Herbs

★★★☆☆

10 Minutes | 0 Minutes | 2 servings

INGREDIENTS

- 2 large zucchinis
- 2 tbsp olive oil
- 2 cloves garlic, minced
- 1/4 cup fresh basil, chopped
- 1/4 cup fresh parsley, chopped
- Salt and pepper to taste
- Grated Parmesan cheese (optional)

INSTRUCTIONS

1. Prepare Zucchini: Spiralize the zucchinis to create noodles and set aside.
2. Cook Garlic: Heat olive oil in a large pan over medium heat. Add minced garlic and cook for 1 minute until fragrant.
3. Cook Zucchini Noodles: Add the zucchini noodles to the pan and sauté for 2-3 minutes until just tender.
4. Add Herbs: Stir in the chopped basil and parsley. Season with salt and pepper to taste.
5. Serve: Transfer to a dark plate and sprinkle with grated Parmesan cheese if desired.

Nutrition Facts : Calories: 120 kcal | Protein: 2 g | Carbs: 6 g | Fat: 10 g | Fiber: 2 g | Sugar: 4 g

37. Grilled Vegetables

★★☆☆☆

10 Minutes   15 Minutes   4 servings

INSTRUCTIONS

1. Prepare Vegetables: Slice zucchinis, bell peppers, and eggplant. Trim the tough ends of the asparagus.
2. Marinate: In a large bowl, combine olive oil, minced garlic, salt, and pepper. Toss the vegetables in the mixture to coat evenly.
3. Grill: Preheat the grill to medium-high heat. Place the vegetables on the grill and cook for about 5-7 minutes per side, or until tender and slightly charred.
4. Serve: Remove from the grill and garnish with fresh herbs. Serve immediately.

INGREDIENTS

- 2 zucchinis, sliced
- 2 bell peppers (paprika), sliced
- 1 eggplant, sliced
- 1 bunch of asparagus
- 3 tbsp olive oil
- 2 cloves garlic, minced
- Salt and pepper to taste
- Fresh herbs (e.g., parsley, thyme) for garnish

Nutrition Facts : Calories: 110 kcal | Protein: 2 g | Carbs: 8 g | Fat: 9 g | Fiber: 3 g | Sugar: 4 g

38. Baked Salmon with Asparagus and Tomatoes

★★★☆☆

10 Minutes   20 Minutes   2 servings

INSTRUCTIONS

1. Preheat Oven: Preheat your oven to 200°C (400°F).
2. Prepare Salmon: Place the salmon fillets on a baking sheet lined with parchment paper. Drizzle 1 tbsp of olive oil over the salmon, then season with garlic powder, dried basil, salt, and pepper.
3. Prepare Vegetables: Arrange the asparagus and cherry tomatoes around the salmon on the baking sheet. Drizzle the remaining olive oil over the vegetables and season with salt and pepper.
4. Bake: Bake in the preheated oven for 15-20 minutes, or until the salmon is cooked through and flakes easily with a fork.
5. Serve: Serve the baked salmon with the roasted asparagus and tomatoes. Garnish with fresh lemon wedges.

INGREDIENTS

- 2 salmon fillets (about 150g each)
- 1 bunch of asparagus, trimmed
- 1 cup cherry tomatoes, halved
- 2 tbsp olive oil
- 1 tsp garlic powder
- 1 tsp dried basil
- Salt and pepper to taste
- Fresh lemon wedges for serving

Nutrition Facts : Calories: 350 kcal | Protein: 30 g | Carbs: 6 g | Fat: 22 g | Fiber: 3 g | Sugar: 4 g

SEAFOOD

39. Salmon Fish Fillet with Fresh Salad and Avocado

★★★★☆

15 Minutes | 15 Minutes | 2 servings

INGREDIENTS

- 2 salmon fillets
- 1 ripe avocado, sliced
- 4 cups mixed salad greens (e.g., lettuce, spinach, arugula)
- 1 cup cherry tomatoes, halved
- 1/2 red onion, thinly sliced
- 2 tbsp olive oil
- 1 tbsp lemon juice
- Salt and pepper to taste
- Fresh dill or parsley for garnish (optional)

INSTRUCTIONS

1. Prepare Salmon: Season the salmon fillets with salt and pepper. Heat a skillet over medium heat and add 1 tbsp of olive oil. Cook the salmon fillets for about 4-5 minutes on each side or until fully cooked and flaky.
2. Prepare Salad: In a large bowl, combine mixed salad greens, sliced avocado, halved cherry tomatoes, and thinly sliced red onion.
3. Make Dressing: In a small bowl, whisk together 1 tbsp olive oil, lemon juice, salt, and pepper.
4. Combine: Place the cooked salmon fillets on top of the salad. Drizzle with the dressing and toss gently to combine.
5. Serve: Garnish with fresh dill or parsley if desired. Serve immediately.

Nutrition Facts: Calories: 480 kcal | Protein: 35 g | Carbs: 12 g | Fat: 35 g | Fiber: 8 g | Sugar: 4 g

40. Crispy Fried Shrimp with Avocado Dip

★★★☆☆

10 Minutes | 20 Minutes | 2 servings

INGREDIENTS

- 500 g shrimp, peeled and deveined
- 2 tbsp olive oil
- 1 tsp garlic powder
- 1 tsp paprika
- Salt and pepper to taste

For the Avocado Dip:

- 2 ripe avocados
- Juice of 1 lemon
- 2 tbsp chopped fresh parsley
- Salt and pepper to taste

INSTRUCTIONS

1. Pat the shrimp dry and season with olive oil, garlic powder, paprika, salt, and pepper.
2. Fry in a pan over medium heat until golden brown and cooked through.
3. For the avocado dip, peel and mash the avocados with lemon juice, parsley, salt, and pepper.
4. Serve the fried shrimp with the avocado dip.

Nutrition Facts: Calories: 280 kcal | Protein: 20 g | Carbs: 10 g | Fat: 18 g | Fiber: 7 g | Sugar: 1 g

41. A Pan of Fish with Vegetables and Herbs

★★★★☆

⏱ 10 Minutes   🍳 20 Minutes   🍴 4 servings

INGREDIENTS

- 4 white fish fillets (e.g., cod or halibut)
- 1 zucchini, sliced
- 1 red bell pepper, sliced
- 1 yellow bell pepper, sliced
- 1 small red onion, sliced
- 2 tablespoons olive oil
- 2 cloves garlic, minced
- 1 lemon, sliced
- Fresh herbs (e.g., parsley, dill, thyme) for garnish
- Salt and pepper to taste

INSTRUCTIONS

1. Preheat the oven to 200 degrees Celsius.
2. Prepare the vegetables: In a large bowl, combine the zucchini, red bell pepper, yellow bell pepper, and red onion. Toss with 1 tablespoon of olive oil, minced garlic, salt, and pepper.
3. Arrange the fish: Place the fish fillets in a large baking dish. Season with salt and pepper. Arrange the prepared vegetables around the fish.
4. Add lemon slices: Place lemon slices on top of the fish fillets and vegetables.
5. Bake: Drizzle the remaining olive oil over the fish and vegetables. Bake in the preheated oven for about 20 minutes or until the fish is cooked through and flakes easily with a fork.
6. Garnish and serve: Remove from the oven and garnish with fresh herbs. Serve hot.

Nutrition Facts: Calories: 250 kcal | Protein: 30 g | Carbs: 10 g | Fat: 10 g | Fiber: 3 g | Sugar: 4 g

42. Shrimps and Avocado Salad with Soft Fried Egg

★★★☆☆

⏱ 15 Minutes   🍳 10 Minutes   🍴 2 servings

INGREDIENTS

- 200 g shrimps or prawns, peeled and deveined
- 2 eggs
- 1 avocado, sliced
- 1 cucumber, sliced
- 2 tomatoes, chopped
- 2 cups mixed salad greens
- 2 tablespoons olive oil
- 1 tablespoon lemon juice
- Salt and pepper to taste
- Fresh dill or parsley for garnish

INSTRUCTIONS

1. In a large bowl, combine the mixed salad greens, sliced cucumber, chopped tomatoes, and avocado slices.
2. Heat 1 tablespoon of olive oil in a pan over medium heat. Add the shrimps or prawns, season with salt and pepper, and cook for about 2-3 minutes on each side until they are pink and opaque. Set aside.
3. In the same pan, add the remaining olive oil and fry the eggs until the whites are set but the yolks are still runny, about 2-3 minutes.
4. Divide the salad mixture between two plates. Top each plate with the cooked shrimps or prawns and a soft fried egg.
5. Drizzle the salad with lemon juice, and season with additional salt and pepper if needed. Garnish with fresh dill or parsley.

Nutrition Facts: Calories: 350 kcal | Protein: 20 g | Carbs: 10 g | Fat: 28 g | Fiber: 7 g | Sugar: 3 g

43. Tuna Salad with Quail Eggs, Lettuce, Red Onion, and Cucumbers

★★★☆☆

15 Minutes | 5 Minutes | 2 servings

INGREDIENTS

- 200 g tuna in olive oil, drained
- 6 quail eggs
- 4 cups mixed lettuce leaves
- 1/2 red onion, thinly sliced
- 1 cucumber, sliced
- 1/2 cup cherry tomatoes, halved
- 1 avocado, sliced
- 1 tbsp capers
- 2 tbsp olive oil
- 1 tbsp lemon juice
- Salt and pepper to taste

INSTRUCTIONS

1. Prepare Quail Eggs: Bring a small pot of water to a boil. Gently add quail eggs and cook for 4 minutes. Transfer eggs to a bowl of cold water to cool. Peel and set aside.
2. Assemble Salad: In a large salad bowl, combine mixed lettuce leaves, thinly sliced red onion, sliced cucumber, cherry tomatoes, and avocado slices.
3. Add Tuna: Flake the drained tuna over the salad.
4. Dress Salad: In a small bowl, whisk together olive oil, lemon juice, salt, and pepper. Drizzle over the salad.
5. Top with Eggs and Capers: Cut the peeled quail eggs in half and arrange them on top of the salad. Sprinkle with capers.
6. Serve: Toss gently to combine and serve immediately.

Nutrition Facts: Calories: 350 kcal | Protein: 25 g | Carbs: 10 g | Fat: 25 g | Fiber: 6 g | Sugar: 4 g

44. Fresh Salad with Fish, Tomatoes, and Lettuce Leaves

★★☆☆☆

15 Minutes | 0 Minutes | 2 servings

INGREDIENTS

- 2 cups mixed lettuce leaves
- 200g grilled or baked fish fillet (e.g., salmon, tuna), flaked
- 1 cup cherry tomatoes, halved
- 1/4 red onion, thinly sliced
- 1/2 avocado, diced
- 2 tbsp olive oil
- 1 tbsp lemon juice
- Salt and pepper to taste
- Fresh dill or parsley for garnish (optional)

INSTRUCTIONS

1. Prepare Salad: In a large bowl, combine mixed lettuce leaves, flaked fish fillet, cherry tomatoes, red onion, and diced avocado.
2. Make Dressing: In a small bowl, whisk together olive oil, lemon juice, salt, and pepper.
3. Combine: Drizzle the dressing over the salad and toss gently to combine.
4. Serve: Garnish with fresh dill or parsley if desired. Serve immediately.

Nutrition Facts: Calories: 320 kcal | Protein: 25 g | Carbs: 8 g | Fat: 22 g | Fiber: 5 g | Sugar: 3 g

45. Japanese Traditional Salad with Grilled Ahi Tuna and Sesame

★★★★★

15 Minutes | **10 Minutes** | **2 servings**

INGREDIENTS

- 200g Ahi tuna steak
- 1 tbsp sesame oil
- 2 tbsp soy sauce (tamari for gluten-free)
- 1 tbsp sesame seeds
- 4 cups mixed greens (e.g., spinach, arugula, lettuce)
- 1/2 cucumber, thinly sliced
- 1 avocado, sliced
- 1/4 red onion, thinly sliced
- 1 tbsp rice vinegar
- 1 tbsp olive oil
- Salt and pepper to taste
- 1 tbsp fresh ginger, grated
- 1 tbsp green onions, chopped (optional)

INSTRUCTIONS

1. Marinate Tuna: In a bowl, combine sesame oil, soy sauce, and grated ginger. Add the Ahi tuna steak and marinate for 10 minutes.
2. Grill Tuna: Heat a grill or pan over medium-high heat. Sear the Ahi tuna steak for about 2-3 minutes on each side for medium-rare. Remove from heat and let it rest before slicing.
3. Prepare Salad: In a large bowl, combine mixed greens, cucumber, avocado, and red onion.
4. Make Dressing: In a small bowl, whisk together rice vinegar, olive oil, salt, and pepper.
5. Combine: Drizzle the dressing over the salad and toss gently to combine. Top with sliced Ahi tuna and sprinkle with sesame seeds.
6. Serve: Garnish with chopped green onions if desired. Serve immediately.

Nutrition Facts: Calories: 350 kcal | Protein: 30 g | Carbs: 10 g | Fat: 22 g | Fiber: 6 g | Sugar: 3 g

46. Salmon Fillet with Broccoli and Almond Crust

★★★★★

20 Minutes | **25 Minutes** | **4 servings**

INGREDIENTS

- 4 salmon fillets
- 2 cups broccoli florets
- 1/4 cup ground almonds
- 2 tbsp melted butter
- 1 tbsp freshly chopped parsley
- Salt and pepper to taste
- Lemon wedges for serving

INSTRUCTIONS

1. Preheat the oven to 200°C and grease a baking dish.
2. Place the salmon fillets on the prepared baking sheet and season with salt, pepper, and lemon juice.
3. Arrange the broccoli florets around the salmon and drizzle with melted butter.
4. Sprinkle ground almonds over the salmon and broccoli and top with parsley.
5. Bake in the preheated oven for about 20-25 minutes until the salmon is cooked through and the almond crust is golden brown.
6. Serve with lemon wedges.

Nutrition Facts: Calories: 320 kcal | Protein: 25 g | Carbs: 5 g | Fat: 22 g | Fiber: 3 g | Sugar: 1 g

47. Steamed Cod with Tomatoes and Olives

★★★☆☆

⏱ 15 Minutes 🍳 20 Minutes 🍴 4 servings

INGREDIENTS

- 4 cod fillets
- 2 tbsp olive oil
- 2 garlic cloves, minced
- 1 onion, chopped
- 1 can (400 g) diced tomatoes
- 1/4 cup pitted olives, sliced
- 1 tbsp capers
- 1/4 cup fresh parsley, chopped
- Salt and pepper to taste

INSTRUCTIONS

1. Heat olive oil in a pan and sauté garlic and onion until soft.
2. Add diced tomatoes, olives, and capers and simmer for about 10 minutes until the sauce thickens slightly.
3. Place the cod fillets on the tomato sauce and season with salt and pepper.
4. Cover the pan and steam the fish for about 8-10 minutes until cooked through.
5. Sprinkle with chopped parsley and serve.

Nutrition Facts : Calories: 320 kcal | Protein: 30 g | Carbs: 10 g | Fat: 18 g | Fiber: 2 g | Sugar: 4 g

48. Pink Salmon Steak Fried and Salad

★★★★☆

⏱ 10 Minutes 🍳 15 Minutes 🍴 2 servings

INGREDIENTS

- 2 pink salmon steaks
- 2 tbsp olive oil
- Salt and pepper to taste
- 1 lemon, sliced
- 2 cups mixed salad greens (e.g., spinach, arugula, lettuce)
- 1/2 cucumber, sliced
- 1/2 red bell pepper, sliced
- 1/4 red onion, thinly sliced
- 1 avocado, sliced
- 2 tbsp olive oil (for dressing)
- 1 tbsp apple cider vinegar
- 1 tsp Dijon mustard

INSTRUCTIONS

1. Cook Salmon: Heat 2 tbsp of olive oil in a pan over medium-high heat. Season the salmon steaks with salt and pepper. Cook the salmon steaks for about 4-5 minutes on each side until they are golden brown and cooked through. Remove from heat and let them rest.
2. Prepare Salad: In a large bowl, combine mixed salad greens, cucumber, red bell pepper, red onion, and avocado.
3. Make Dressing: In a small bowl, whisk together 2 tbsp olive oil, apple cider vinegar, Dijon mustard, salt, and pepper.
4. Combine: Drizzle the dressing over the salad and toss gently to combine.
5. Serve: Serve the salad with the fried salmon steaks on top, garnished with lemon slices.

Nutrition Facts: Calories: 450 kcal | Protein: 30 g | Carbs: 10 g | Fat: 34 g | Fiber: 6 g | Sugar: 3 g

49. Fried Broccoli with Garlic and Shrimp

★★★☆☆

15 Minutes 10 Minutes 2 servings

INGREDIENTS

- 2 cups broccoli florets
- 200 g shrimp, peeled and deveined
- 4 garlic cloves, minced
- 2 tbsp olive oil
- 1 tbsp soy sauce (or tamari for gluten-free)
- 1 tbsp fish sauce
- 1 tsp chili flakes (optional)
- Salt and pepper to taste
- Fresh cilantro for garnish

INSTRUCTIONS

1. Prepare Ingredients: Rinse the broccoli and shrimp. Mince the garlic.
2. Cook Broccoli: Heat 1 tbsp of olive oil in a large pan or wok over medium-high heat. Add the broccoli and stir-fry for about 3-4 minutes until it starts to become tender. Remove from the pan and set aside.
3. Cook Shrimp: In the same pan, add the remaining 1 tbsp of olive oil. Add the minced garlic and stir-fry for about 30 seconds until fragrant. Add the shrimp and cook for about 2-3 minutes until pink and cooked through.
4. Combine and Season: Return the broccoli to the pan. Add soy sauce, fish sauce, chili flakes (if using), salt, and pepper. Stir well to combine and cook for another 2 minutes until everything is heated through.
5. Serve: Garnish with fresh cilantro and serve immediately.

Nutrition Facts: Calories: 250 kcal | Protein: 25 g | Carbs: 8 g | Fat: 14 g | Fiber: 3 g | Sugar: 2 g

50. Pan-Fried Tuna with Sesame Seeds

★★★★☆

10 Minutes 15 Minutes 2 servings

INGREDIENTS

- 4 tuna steaks
- 3 tbsp soy sauce
- 2 tbsp sesame oil
- 2 tbsp sesame seeds
- 2 garlic cloves, minced
- Spring onions for garnish
- Salt and pepper to taste

INSTRUCTIONS

1. Marinate the tuna steaks in soy sauce and sesame oil for about 15 minutes.
2. Heat a pan over medium heat and cook the tuna steaks for about 3-4 minutes per side until slightly crispy outside and pink inside.
3. Add minced garlic and sesame seeds to the pan and cook for about 1-2 minutes until fragrant and lightly toasted.
4. Garnish with spring onions and serve.

Nutrition Facts : Calories: 280 kcal | Protein: 30 g | Carbs: 2 g | Fat: 16 g | Fiber: 1 g | Sugar: 0 g

51. Baked Scallops with Herb Butter

★★★☆☆

🕐 10 Minutes   🍳 12 Minutes   🍴 4 servings

INGREDIENTS

- 12 scallops
- 4 tbsp butter, melted
- 2 garlic cloves, minced
- 2 tbsp fresh parsley, chopped
- Juice and zest of 1 lemon
- Salt and pepper to taste

INSTRUCTIONS

1. Preheat the oven to 200°C and lightly grease a baking dish.
2. Pat the scallops dry and place them in the prepared baking dish.
3. Mix melted butter with garlic, parsley, lemon juice, and zest, and drizzle over the scallops.
4. Bake the scallops for about 10-12 minutes until cooked through and lightly browned.
5. Drizzle with additional lemon juice and serve immediately.

Nutrition Facts : Calories: 220 kcal | Protein: 20 g | Carbs: 3 g | Fat: 14 g | Fiber: 1 g | Sugar: 0 g

---

52. Salmon and Avocado Salad

★★★★☆

🕐 15 Minutes   🍳 10 Minutes   🍴 2 servings

INGREDIENTS

- 200 g grilled salmon fillet, flaked
- 1 avocado, diced
- 2 cups mixed salad greens
- 1/2 cup cherry tomatoes, halved
- 1/4 red onion, thinly sliced
- 2 tbsp olive oil
- Juice of 1 lemon
- Salt and pepper to taste

INSTRUCTIONS

1. Prepare the Ingredients: In a large bowl, combine the mixed salad greens, flaked salmon, diced avocado, cherry tomatoes, and thinly sliced red onion.
2. Make the Dressing: In a small bowl, whisk together the olive oil, lemon juice, salt, and pepper.
3. Assemble the Salad: Drizzle the dressing over the salad and toss gently to combine.
4. Serve: Serve immediately as a nutritious keto-friendly meal.

Nutrition Facts : Calories: 350 kcal | Protein: 25 g | Carbs: 10 g | Fat: 25 g | Fiber: 6 g | Sugar: 4 g

53. Seared Tuna with Sesame Crust

★★★☆☆

10 Minutes | 5 Minutes | 2 servings

INGREDIENTS

- 2 tuna steaks (about 150g each)
- 2 tbsp sesame seeds
- 1 tbsp black sesame seeds
- 2 tbsp soy sauce
- 1 tbsp sesame oil
- 1 tsp grated ginger
- 1 garlic clove, minced
- Salt and pepper to taste
- Fresh cilantro for garnish (optional)
- Lime wedges for serving

INSTRUCTIONS

1. Prepare Marinade: In a small bowl, combine soy sauce, sesame oil, grated ginger, and minced garlic.
2. Marinate Tuna: Place tuna steaks in the marinade and let sit for 5 minutes, turning occasionally.
3. Prepare Sesame Coating: On a plate, mix together the sesame seeds and black sesame seeds.
4. Coat Tuna: Remove tuna steaks from the marinade and press each side into the sesame seed mixture to coat.
5. Sear Tuna: Heat a non-stick skillet over medium-high heat. Sear the tuna steaks for about 1-2 minutes on each side, depending on desired doneness.
6. Serve: Slice the tuna and serve with lime wedges. Garnish with fresh cilantro if desired.

Nutrition Facts: Calories: 280 kcal | Protein: 40 g | Carbs: 2 g | Fat: 12 g | Fiber: 1 g | Sugar: 0 g

54. Avocado Oil-Based Aioli Sauce

★★☆☆☆

10 Minutes | 0 Minutes | 4 servings

INGREDIENTS

- 1 large egg yolk
- 1 tsp Dijon mustard
- 1 clove garlic, minced
- 1 tbsp lemon juice
- 1/2 cup avocado oil
- Salt and pepper to taste

INSTRUCTIONS

1. Prepare Ingredients: In a medium bowl, whisk together the egg yolk, Dijon mustard, minced garlic, and lemon juice.
2. Emulsify: Slowly drizzle in the avocado oil while continuously whisking until the mixture thickens and emulsifies into a creamy sauce.
3. Season: Add salt and pepper to taste and mix well.
4. Serve: Transfer to a serving dish and pair with your favorite seafood or use as a dip for vegetables.

Nutrition Facts: Calories: 150 kcal | Protein: 1 g | Carbs: 1 g | Fat: 15 g | Fiber: 0 g | Sugar: 0 g

55. Salmon Cooked with Asparagus

★★★☆☆

🕐 10 Minutes   🍳 15 Minutes   🍴 2 servings

INGREDIENTS

- 2 salmon fillets
- 1 bunch of asparagus, trimmed
- 2 tbsp olive oil
- 1 lemon, sliced
- 2 cloves garlic, minced
- Salt and pepper to taste
- Fresh dill for garnish

INSTRUCTIONS

1. Preheat Oven: Preheat your oven to 200°C (400°F).
2. Prepare Salmon and Asparagus: Place the salmon fillets and asparagus on a baking sheet. Drizzle with olive oil and sprinkle with minced garlic, salt, and pepper.
3. Add Lemon: Arrange lemon slices over the salmon and asparagus.
4. Bake: Bake in the preheated oven for 12-15 minutes, or until the salmon is cooked through and the asparagus is tender.
5. Garnish and Serve: Garnish with fresh dill before serving.

Nutrition Facts: Calories: 350 kcal | Protein: 30 g | Carbs: 5 g | Fat: 25 g | Fiber: 2 g | Sugar: 2 g

56. Steamed Salmon Steak with Vegetables

★★★★☆

🕐 10 Minutes   🍳 20 Minutes   🍴 2 servings

INGREDIENTS

- 2 salmon steaks
- 1 cup broccoli florets
- 1 cup sliced zucchini
- 1 cup sliced carrots
- 2 tbsp olive oil
- Juice of 1 lemon
- Salt and pepper to taste
- Fresh dill for garnish

INSTRUCTIONS

1. Prepare the Ingredients: Season the salmon steaks with salt, pepper, and lemon juice. Set aside.
2. Steam the Vegetables: In a steamer, place the broccoli florets, sliced zucchini, and sliced carrots. Steam for about 10-15 minutes until tender.
3. Steam the Salmon: Add the salmon steaks to the steamer and steam for another 10-12 minutes until cooked through.
4. Serve: Arrange the steamed vegetables on a plate, place the steamed salmon steak on top, and drizzle with olive oil. Garnish with fresh dill.
5. Enjoy: Serve immediately while hot.

Nutrition Facts : Calories: 350 kcal | Protein: 25 g | Carbs: 10 g | Fat: 25 g | Fiber: 5 g | Sugar: 4 g

MEAT

57. Chicken Fillet with Quail Eggs, Avocado, Spinach, and Walnuts

★★★☆☆

⏱ 15 Minutes 🍳 20 Minutes 🍴 2 servings

INGREDIENTS

- 2 chicken fillets
- 6 quail eggs
- 1 ripe avocado, sliced
- 2 cups fresh spinach leaves
- 1/4 cup walnuts, chopped
- 2 tbsp olive oil
- Salt and pepper to taste
- Optional: lemon wedges for serving

INSTRUCTIONS

1. Prepare Chicken: Season the chicken fillets with salt and pepper. Heat 1 tbsp of olive oil in a pan over medium heat. Cook the chicken fillets for 5-7 minutes on each side, or until cooked through and golden brown. Remove from the pan and let rest for a few minutes before slicing.
2. Cook Quail Eggs: Bring a small pot of water to a gentle boil. Add the quail eggs and cook for 4 minutes. Remove and place in cold water. Once cool, peel and set aside.
3. Sauté Spinach: In the same pan used for the chicken, add 1 tbsp of olive oil and the spinach. Cook until just wilted, about 2-3 minutes. Season with salt and pepper.
4. Assemble: Arrange the sliced chicken, quail eggs, avocado slices, and sautéed spinach on a serving plate. Sprinkle with chopped walnuts.
5. Serve: Optional - squeeze lemon juice over the dish for added flavor. Serve immediately.

Nutrition Facts: Calories: 450 kcal | Protein: 35 g | Carbs: 6 g | Fat: 30 g | Fiber: 7 g | Sugar: 1 g

58. Salad with Spinach, Arugula, and Sliced Beef Steak

★★★★☆

⏱ 10 Minutes 🍳 15 Minutes 🍴 2 servings

INGREDIENTS

- 200g beef steak
- 1 tbsp olive oil
- Salt and pepper to taste
- 2 cups fresh spinach leaves
- 2 cups fresh arugula leaves
- 1/2 avocado, sliced
- 1/4 red onion, thinly sliced
- 1/2 cup cherry tomatoes, halved
- 2 tbsp balsamic vinegar
- 2 tbsp extra virgin olive oil
- 1 tsp Dijon mustard
- Salt and pepper to taste

INSTRUCTIONS

1. Prepare the Steak: Season the beef steak with salt and pepper.
2. Cook the Steak: Heat the olive oil in a skillet over medium-high heat. Cook the steak for about 4-5 minutes on each side for medium-rare, or until desired doneness. Remove from skillet and let rest for a few minutes, then slice thinly.
3. Prepare the Salad: In a large bowl, combine spinach, arugula, avocado, red onion, and cherry tomatoes.
4. Make the Dressing: In a small bowl, whisk together balsamic vinegar, extra virgin olive oil, Dijon mustard, salt, and pepper.
5. Assemble the Salad: Drizzle the dressing over the salad and toss to combine. Top with sliced beef steak.
6. Serve: Divide the salad between two plates and serve immediately.

Nutrition Facts: Calories: 380 kcal | Protein: 25 g | Carbs: 8 g | Fat: 28 g | Fiber: 5 g | Sugar: 3 g

59. Beefsteak with Red Peppercorn and Avocado

★★★☆☆

⏱ 10 Minutes | 🍳 15 Minutes | 🍴 2 servings

INGREDIENTS

- 2 beefsteak cuts (about 200g each)
- 1 tbsp olive oil
- Salt and pepper to taste
- 1 tbsp red peppercorns
- 1 ripe avocado, sliced
- Fresh cilantro or parsley for garnish (optional)
- Lime wedges for serving

INSTRUCTIONS

1. Prepare the Steak: Season the beefsteak cuts with salt and pepper.
2. Heat the Oil: In a large skillet, heat the olive oil over medium-high heat.
3. Cook the Steak: Add the beefsteaks to the skillet and cook for about 4-5 minutes on each side for medium-rare, or until desired doneness is reached.
4. Rest the Steak: Remove the steaks from the skillet and let rest for a few minutes.
5. Serve: Slice the steaks and arrange on a plate. Garnish with red peppercorns and avocado slices.
6. Garnish: Optionally, garnish with fresh cilantro or parsley and serve with lime wedges.

Nutrition Facts : Calories: 450 kcal | Protein: 35 g | Carbs: 4 g | Fat: 32 g | Fiber: 5 g | Sugar: 1 g

60. Grilled Steak and Pear Salad with Blue Cheese

★★★☆☆

⏱ 15 Minutes | 🍳 10 Minutes | 🍴 4 servings

INGREDIENTS

- 4 sirloin steaks (about 6 ounces each)
- Salt and pepper to taste
- 2 tablespoons olive oil
- 2 ripe pears, sliced
- 4 cups mixed salad greens
- 1/2 cup crumbled blue cheese
- 1/4 cup walnuts, toasted
- 3 tablespoons balsamic vinegar

INSTRUCTIONS

1. Preheat the grill to high heat.
2. Season steaks with salt and pepper and brush with 1 tablespoon olive oil.
3. Grill steaks for about 4-5 minutes per side for medium-rare, or until they reach the desired doneness.
4. Let steaks rest for a few minutes, then slice thinly.
5. In a large salad bowl, combine mixed greens, sliced pears, crumbled blue cheese, and toasted walnuts.
6. Whisk together balsamic vinegar and remaining olive oil, drizzle over the salad.
7. Top salad with sliced grilled steak and serve immediately.

Nutritional : Calories: 490 kcal | Protein: 36 g | Carbohydrates: 18 g | Fat: 32 g | Fiber: 3 g | Sugar: 12 g

61. Chicken with Onions, Capers, and Lemon Zest

★★★★★

🕐 10 Minutes   🍳 20 Minutes   🍴 4 servings

INGREDIENTS

- 4 chicken breasts, boneless and skinless
- Salt and pepper to taste
- 2 tablespoons olive oil
- 1 large onion, thinly sliced
- 2 tablespoons capers, rinsed
- 1 lemon, zest and juice
- Fresh parsley, chopped for garnish

INSTRUCTIONS

1. Season chicken breasts with salt and pepper.
2. Heat olive oil in a large skillet over medium-high heat.
3. Add chicken and cook until golden brown on both sides and cooked through, about 6-7 minutes per side.
4. Remove chicken from skillet and set aside.
5. In the same skillet, add onions and sauté until soft and caramelized, about 8 minutes.
6. Add capers and lemon zest, cook for an additional 2 minutes.
7. Return chicken to the skillet, squeeze over lemon juice, and heat through.
8. Garnish with fresh parsley before serving.

Nutritional : Calories: 300 kcal | Protein: 26 g | Carbohydrates: 6 g | Fat: 18 g | Fiber: 1 g | Sugar: 2 g

62. Lamb Chops with Pesto Sauce

★★★★★

🕐 15 Minutes   🍳 10 Minutes   🍴 4 servings

INGREDIENTS

- 8 lamb chops
- Salt and pepper to taste
- 2 tablespoons olive oil
- 1/2 cup homemade or store-bought pesto sauce

INSTRUCTIONS

1. Season lamb chops with salt and pepper.
2. Heat olive oil in a large skillet over medium-high heat.
3. Add lamb chops and cook for about 3-4 minutes per side for medium-rare, or until they reach the desired level of doneness.
4. Remove from heat and let rest for a few minutes.
5. Serve lamb chops with a generous dollop of pesto sauce on top.

Nutritional Information: Calories: 400 kcal | Protein: 35 g | Carbohydrates: 2 g | Fat: 28 g | Fiber: 0.5 g

63. Grilled Meat with Blueberry Sauce

★★★☆☆

15 Minutes | 15 Minutes | 4 servings

INGREDIENTS

- 4 steaks (such as ribeye or sirloin, about 6 ounces each)
- Salt and pepper to taste
- 1 tablespoon olive oil
- 1 cup fresh blueberries
- 2 tablespoons balsamic vinegar
- 1 tablespoon honey
- 1 teaspoon fresh rosemary, minced

INSTRUCTIONS

1. Preheat grill to high heat.
2. Season steaks with salt and pepper and brush with olive oil.
3. Grill steaks to desired doneness, about 5-7 minutes per side for medium-rare.
4. While the steaks are grilling, combine blueberries, balsamic vinegar, honey, and rosemary in a small saucepan over medium heat.
5. Cook until blueberries have burst and the sauce has thickened, about 10 minutes.
6. Serve the grilled steaks drizzled with the blueberry sauce.

Nutritional : Calories: 420 kcal | Protein: 35 g | Carbohydrates: 12 g | Fat: 26 g | Fiber: 1 g | Sugar: 10 g

64. Chicken with Lemon Slices

★★★☆☆

10 Minutes | 25 Minutes | 4 servings

INGREDIENTS

- 4 chicken breasts (boneless, skinless)
- 2 lemons, thinly sliced
- 2 tablespoons olive oil
- Salt and pepper to taste
- 1 teaspoon dried thyme

INSTRUCTIONS

1. Preheat the oven to 375°F (190°C).
2. Rub each chicken breast with olive oil, then season generously with salt, pepper, and dried thyme.
3. Arrange lemon slices on the bottom of a baking dish and place the seasoned chicken breasts on top.
4. Bake in the preheated oven for about 25 minutes, or until the chicken is cooked through and juices run clear.
5. Serve the chicken garnished with additional fresh thyme if desired.

Nutritional : Calories: 220 kcal | Protein: 26 g | Carbohydrates: 5 g | Fat: 11 g | Fiber: 1 g | Sugar: 1 g

65. Grilled Chicken Breast and Spinach Salad with Avocado, Tomatoes, and Sesame Seeds

★★★☆☆

15 Minutes   15 Minutes   2 servings

INGREDIENTS

- 2 chicken breasts
- 2 cups fresh spinach leaves
- 1 ripe avocado, sliced
- 1 cup cherry tomatoes, halved
- 2 tbsp sesame seeds
- 2 tbsp olive oil
- 1 tbsp lemon juice
- Salt and pepper to taste

INSTRUCTIONS

1. Prepare Chicken: Season the chicken breasts with salt and pepper. Heat a grill pan over medium heat and grill the chicken breasts for about 6-7 minutes on each side or until fully cooked.
2. Prepare Salad: In a large bowl, combine fresh spinach leaves, sliced avocado, and halved cherry tomatoes.
3. Toast Sesame Seeds: In a small skillet over medium heat, toast the sesame seeds for 2-3 minutes until golden brown. Set aside.
4. Make Dressing: In a small bowl, whisk together olive oil, lemon juice, salt, and pepper.
5. Combine: Slice the grilled chicken breasts and add them to the salad. Drizzle with the dressing and toss gently to combine.
6. Serve: Sprinkle toasted sesame seeds on top and serve immediately.

Nutrition Facts: Calories: 420 kcal | Protein: 30 g | Carbs: 10 g | Fat: 30 g | Fiber: 8 g | Sugar: 3 g

66. Baked Scallops with Herb Butter

★★★☆☆

10 Minutes   12 Minutes   4 servings

INGREDIENTS

- 12 scallops
- 4 tbsp butter, melted
- 2 garlic cloves, finely chopped
- 2 tbsp fresh parsley, chopped
- Juice and zest of 1 lemon
- Salt and pepper to taste

INSTRUCTIONS

1. Preheat the oven to 200°C and lightly grease a baking dish.
2. Pat the scallops dry and place them in the prepared baking dish.
3. Mix the melted butter with garlic, parsley, lemon juice, and zest, then drizzle over the scallops.
4. Bake the scallops for about 10-12 minutes until they are cooked through and lightly browned.
5. Drizzle with additional lemon juice and serve immediately.

Nutrition Facts: Calories: 220 kcal | Protein: 20 g | Carbs: 3 g | Fat: 14 g | Fiber: 1 g | Sugar: 0 g

67. Keto Salad with Chicken Meat Sous Vide, Tomatoes, Cucumbers, and Avocado

★★★★★

15 Minutes | 15 Minutes | 2 servings

INGREDIENTS

- 2 chicken breasts (sous vide)
- 1 avocado, sliced
- 1 cup cherry tomatoes, halved
- 1 cup cucumber, sliced
- 4 cups mixed greens (lettuce, spinach, arugula)
- 2 tbsp olive oil
- 1 tbsp lemon juice
- Salt and pepper to taste
- Fresh herbs (e.g., parsley, cilantro) for garnish

INSTRUCTIONS

1. Prepare Chicken Sous Vide: Season the chicken breasts with salt and pepper. Vacuum-seal the chicken breasts and cook them in a sous vide water bath at 60°C (140°F) for 1.5 to 2 hours. Once cooked, remove from the bag and sear in a hot pan for 1-2 minutes on each side until browned. Let cool slightly, then slice.
2. Prepare Vegetables: While the chicken is cooking, wash and prepare the avocado, cherry tomatoes, cucumber, and mixed greens.
3. Make Dressing: In a small bowl, whisk together olive oil, lemon juice, salt, and pepper.
4. Assemble Salad: In two bowls, distribute the mixed greens evenly. Arrange the avocado, cherry tomatoes, cucumber, and sliced chicken on top of the greens.
5. Add Dressing and Serve: Drizzle the dressing over the salads. Garnish with fresh herbs and serve immediately.

Nutrition Facts: Calories: 450 kcal | Protein: 30 g | Carbs: 12 g | Fat: 30 g | Fiber: 7 g | Sugar: 4 g

68. Chicken Salad with Avocado, Spinach, and Blueberries

★★★★★

15 Minutes | 10 Minutes | 2 servings

INGREDIENTS

- 200 g grilled chicken breast, sliced
- 1 avocado, diced
- 2 cups fresh spinach leaves
- 1/2 cup fresh blueberries
- 1/4 cup chopped walnuts
- 2 tbsp olive oil
- Juice of 1 lemon
- Salt and pepper to taste

INSTRUCTIONS

1. Prepare the Ingredients: In a large bowl, combine the spinach, grilled chicken breast, diced avocado, fresh blueberries, and chopped walnuts.
2. Make the Dressing: In a small bowl, whisk together the olive oil, lemon juice, salt, and pepper.
3. Assemble the Salad: Drizzle the dressing over the salad and toss gently to combine.
4. Serve: Serve immediately as a nutritious keto-friendly meal.

Nutrition Facts: Calories: 400 kcal | Protein: 25 g | Carbs: 12 g | Fat: 30 g | Fiber: 7 g | Sugar: 5 g

69. Steak with Green Garnish

★★★☆☆

10 Minutes   15 Minutes   2 servings

INGREDIENTS

- 2 steaks (ribeye, sirloin, or your choice)
- 2 tbsp olive oil
- Salt and pepper to taste
- 2 garlic cloves, minced
- Fresh herbs for garnish (parsley, cilantro, or your choice)
- Lemon wedge for serving (optional)

INSTRUCTIONS

1. Prepare the Steaks: Pat the steaks dry with a paper towel. Rub both sides with olive oil and season generously with salt and pepper.
2. Cook the Steaks: Heat a large skillet over medium-high heat. Add the minced garlic and cook for 1 minute until fragrant. Add the steaks and cook for about 4-5 minutes on each side for medium-rare, or to your desired doneness.
3. Rest and Garnish: Remove the steaks from the skillet and let them rest for 5 minutes. Garnish with fresh herbs and a squeeze of lemon juice if desired.
4. Serve: Serve the steaks hot, with additional fresh herbs on top for garnish.

Nutrition Facts: Calories: 450 kcal | Protein: 30 g | Carbs: 1 g | Fat: 35 g | Fiber: 0 g | Sugar: 0 g

70. Barbecue Pork Ribs

★★★☆☆

15 Minutes   180 Minutes   4 servings

INGREDIENTS

- 1 rack of pork ribs
- 2 tbsp olive oil
- Salt and pepper to taste
- 1 tbsp smoked paprika
- 1 tbsp garlic powder
- 1 tbsp onion powder
- 1 tsp ground cumin
- 1 cup sugar-free barbecue sauce

INSTRUCTIONS

1. Prepare the Ribs: Preheat your grill to medium-low heat. Pat the ribs dry with a paper towel. Rub both sides with olive oil, then season generously with salt, pepper, smoked paprika, garlic powder, onion powder, and ground cumin.
2. Grill the Ribs: Place the ribs on the grill and cook for about 2.5 to 3 hours, maintaining a temperature of 225-250°F (110-120°C). Turn the ribs occasionally to ensure even cooking.
3. Apply Barbecue Sauce: During the last 30 minutes of cooking, brush the ribs with sugar-free barbecue sauce. Continue to turn and baste the ribs every 10 minutes.
4. Rest and Serve: Remove the ribs from the grill and let them rest for 10 minutes before cutting into individual ribs. Serve hot with additional barbecue sauce on the side if desired.

Nutrition Facts : Calories: 500 kcal | Protein: 40 g | Carbs: 5 g | Fat: 35 g | Fiber: 1 g | Sugar: 2 g

71. Pear Appetizer with Jamon, Prosciutto Ham, and Blue Cheese

★★☆☆☆

10 Minutes | 0 Minutes | 4 servings

INGREDIENTS

- 2 ripe pears, sliced thinly
- 8 slices of jamon or prosciutto ham
- 100 g blue cheese, crumbled
- Fresh arugula for garnish
- 2 tbsp olive oil
- 1 tbsp balsamic vinegar
- Salt and pepper to taste

INSTRUCTIONS

1. Prepare the Pears: Slice the pears thinly and arrange them on a serving platter.
2. Assemble the Appetizer: Place a slice of jamon or prosciutto ham on top of each pear slice.
3. Add the Cheese: Crumble the blue cheese over the ham and pear slices.
4. Garnish and Dress: Garnish with fresh arugula. Drizzle olive oil and balsamic vinegar over the top. Season with salt and pepper to taste.
5. Serve: Serve immediately as a fresh, light appetizer.

Nutrition Facts: Calories: 250 kcal | Protein: 12 g | Carbs: 10 g | Fat: 18 g | Fiber: 2 g | Sugar: 6 g

72. Fresh Chicken Salad with Seasonings

★★★☆☆

15 Minutes | 10 Minutes | 2 servings

INGREDIENTS

- 2 chicken breasts, cooked and shredded
- 2 cups mixed greens (e.g., arugula, spinach, lettuce)
- 1 avocado, diced
- 1/2 red onion, thinly sliced
- 1/2 cup cherry tomatoes, halved
- 2 tbsp olive oil
- 1 tbsp apple cider vinegar
- 1 tsp Dijon mustard
- Salt and pepper to taste
- Fresh herbs (e.g., parsley, cilantro) for garnish

INSTRUCTIONS

1. Prepare the Salad: In a large salad bowl, combine mixed greens, diced avocado, thinly sliced red onion, and cherry tomatoes.
2. Add the Chicken: Add the shredded chicken breasts to the salad.
3. Make the Dressing: In a small bowl, whisk together olive oil, apple cider vinegar, Dijon mustard, salt, and pepper.
4. Dress the Salad: Pour the dressing over the salad and toss gently to combine.
5. Garnish and Serve: Garnish with fresh herbs and serve immediately.

Nutrition Facts: Calories: 350 kcal | Protein: 30 g | Carbs: 10 g | Fat: 22 g | Fiber: 5 g | Sugar: 3 g

73. Meatballs with Vegetables

★★★☆☆

🕐 15 Minutes   🍳 25 Minutes   🍴 4 servings

INGREDIENTS

- 500g ground beef
- 1 egg
- 1/4 cup almond flour
- 2 cloves garlic, minced
- 1/4 cup grated Parmesan cheese
- 1 tbsp fresh parsley, chopped
- Salt and pepper to taste
- 1 zucchini, sliced
- 1 bell pepper, chopped
- 1 cup cherry tomatoes
- 2 tbsp olive oil
- 1 tsp Italian seasoning

INSTRUCTIONS

1. Preheat Oven: Preheat your oven to 200°C (400°F).
2. Prepare Meatballs: In a bowl, combine ground beef, egg, almond flour, minced garlic, Parmesan cheese, chopped parsley, salt, and pepper. Mix well and form into meatballs.
3. Arrange Vegetables: Place the zucchini, bell pepper, and cherry tomatoes on a baking sheet. Drizzle with olive oil and sprinkle with Italian seasoning, salt, and pepper.
4. Add Meatballs: Place the meatballs on the same baking sheet with the vegetables.
5. Bake: Bake in the preheated oven for 20-25 minutes, or until the meatballs are cooked through and the vegetables are tender.
6. Serve: Serve the meatballs with the roasted vegetables.

Nutrition Facts: Calories: 350 kcal | Protein: 25 g | Carbs: 8 g | Fat: 25 g | Fiber: 3 g | Sugar: 4 g

74. Meatballs with Tomato Sauce and Basil Garnish

★★★☆☆

🕐 15 Minutes   🍳 10 Minutes   🍴 2 servings

INGREDIENTS

- 500g ground beef
- 1 egg
- 1/4 cup almond flour
- 2 cloves garlic, minced
- 1/4 cup grated Parmesan cheese
- 1 tbsp fresh parsley, chopped
- Salt and pepper to taste
- 2 cups sugar-free tomato sauce
- 1 tbsp olive oil
- Fresh basil leaves for garnish

INSTRUCTIONS

1. Preheat Oven: Preheat your oven to 200°C (400°F).
2. Prepare Meatballs: In a bowl, combine ground beef, egg, almond flour, minced garlic, Parmesan cheese, chopped parsley, salt, and pepper. Mix well and form into meatballs.
3. Cook Meatballs: In a large oven-safe skillet, heat the olive oil over medium heat. Add the meatballs and cook until they are browned on all sides.
4. Add Tomato Sauce: Pour the sugar-free tomato sauce over the meatballs.
5. Bake: Transfer the skillet to the preheated oven and bake for 20-25 minutes, or until the meatballs are cooked through.
6. Garnish and Serve: Garnish with fresh basil leaves and serve hot.

Nutrition Facts: Calories: 320 kcal | Protein: 28 g | Carbs: 6 g | Fat: 20 g | Fiber: 2 g | Sugar: 3 g

VEGAN

75. Summer Salad with Arugula, Strawberry, and Nuts

★★☆☆☆

10 Minutes | 0 Minutes | 2 servings

INGREDIENTS

- 4 cups arugula
- 1/2 cup strawberries, sliced
- 1/4 cup nuts (e.g., almonds, walnuts), chopped
- 2 tbsp olive oil
- 1 tbsp balsamic vinegar
- Salt and pepper to taste

INSTRUCTIONS

1. Prepare Ingredients: Wash the arugula and strawberries. Slice the strawberries and chop the nuts.
2. Make Dressing: In a small bowl, whisk together olive oil, balsamic vinegar, salt, and pepper.
3. Assemble Salad: In two bowls, distribute the arugula evenly. Arrange the sliced strawberries and chopped nuts on top.
4. Add Dressing and Serve: Drizzle the dressing over the salads. Toss gently and serve immediately.

Nutrition Facts: Calories: 200 kcal | Protein: 4 g | Carbs: 8 g | Fat: 18 g | Fiber: 4 g | Sugar: 4 g

76. Vegetable Salad

★★☆☆☆

10 Minutes | 0 Minutes | 2 servings

INGREDIENTS

- 1 cup mixed greens (lettuce, spinach, arugula)
- 1/2 cup cherry tomatoes, halved
- 1/2 cucumber, sliced
- 1/4 red onion, thinly sliced
- 1/4 avocado, diced
- 2 tbsp olive oil
- 1 tbsp apple cider vinegar
- Salt and pepper to taste

INSTRUCTIONS

1. Prepare Vegetables: Wash and prepare all vegetables as indicated.
2. Combine Salad: In a large bowl, combine mixed greens, cherry tomatoes, cucumber, red onion, and avocado.
3. Dress Salad: Drizzle olive oil and apple cider vinegar over the salad. Season with salt and pepper to taste.
4. Toss and Serve: Toss the salad until all ingredients are well coated with the dressing. Serve immediately.

Nutrition Facts: Calories: 180 kcal | Protein: 2 g | Carbs: 8 g | Fat: 16 g | Fiber: 4 g | Sugar: 3 g

77. Fresh Radish and Greens Salad with Seeds

★★☆☆☆

15 Minutes | 0 Minutes | 2 servings

INGREDIENTS

- 1 cup fresh radishes, thinly sliced
- 2 cups arugula
- 1 cup beets, grated or thinly sliced
- 1 cup Swiss chard, chopped
- 2 tbsp sunflower seeds
- 1 tbsp flax seeds
- 1 tbsp sesame seeds
- 2 tbsp olive oil
- 1 tbsp apple cider vinegar
- Salt and pepper to taste

INSTRUCTIONS

1. Prepare Vegetables: In a large bowl, combine the sliced radishes, arugula, grated beets, and chopped Swiss chard.
2. Add Seeds: Sprinkle sunflower seeds, flax seeds, and sesame seeds over the vegetables.
3. Make Dressing: In a small bowl, whisk together olive oil, apple cider vinegar, salt, and pepper.
4. Combine: Drizzle the dressing over the salad and toss gently to combine.
5. Serve: Serve immediately as a fresh, nutrient-packed keto-friendly salad.

Nutrition Facts : Calories: 220 kcal | Protein: 6 g | Carbs: 10 g | Fat: 18 g | Fiber: 5 g | Sugar: 4 g

78. Tofu with Broccoli and Peppers

★★☆☆☆

10 Minutes | 0 Minutes | 2 servings

INGREDIENTS

- 200 g firm tofu, cubed
- 1 cup broccoli florets
- 1 red bell pepper, sliced
- 2 tbsp olive oil
- 1 tbsp soy sauce (or tamari for gluten-free)
- 1 clove garlic, minced
- 1/2 tsp ground ginger
- Salt and pepper to taste
- 1 tbsp sesame seeds (optional)

INSTRUCTIONS

1. Prepare Tofu: Press the tofu to remove excess moisture and cut it into cubes.
2. Stir-Fry Tofu: Heat 1 tbsp of olive oil in a large pan over medium heat. Add the tofu and cook until golden brown on all sides. Remove from pan and set aside.
3. Cook Vegetables: In the same pan, heat the remaining olive oil. Add the minced garlic and ginger, cook for 1 minute until fragrant.
4. Add Broccoli and Peppers: Add the broccoli florets and sliced red bell pepper. Stir-fry for 5-7 minutes until the vegetables are tender-crisp.
5. Combine and Season: Return the tofu to the pan. Add soy sauce, salt, and pepper. Stir well to combine and heat through.
6. Serve: Transfer to a serving bowl and sprinkle with sesame seeds if desired.

Nutrition Facts: Calories: 220 kcal | Protein: 12 g | Carbs: 10 g | Fat: 16 g | Fiber: 4 g | Sugar: 3 g

79. Pan of Broccoli and Carrots

★★★★☆

10 Minutes | 15 Minutes | 4 servings

INGREDIENTS

- 2 cups broccoli florets
- 1 cup sliced carrots (use sparingly to keep it keto-friendly)
- 2 tbsp olive oil
- 2 cloves garlic, minced
- Salt and pepper to taste
- 1 tsp dried thyme or fresh thyme leaves

INSTRUCTIONS

1. Prepare Vegetables: Wash and cut broccoli into florets. Peel and thinly slice the carrots.
2. Cook Vegetables: Heat olive oil in a large pan over medium heat. Add minced garlic and sauté for 1 minute until fragrant. Add broccoli florets and sliced carrots to the pan.
3. Season with salt, pepper, and thyme. Cook, stirring occasionally, for 10-15 minutes or until vegetables are tender.
4. Serve: Transfer the cooked vegetables to a serving dish. Serve warm as a side dish.

Nutrition Facts : Calories: 90 kcal | Protein: 2 g | Carbs: 7 g | Fat: 7 g | Fiber: 3 g | Sugar: 2 g

80. Keto-Friendly Salad Bowl with Avocado, Boiled Egg, Pumpkin, and Arugula

★★☆☆☆

15 Minutes | 20 Minutes | 2 servings

INGREDIENTS

- 2 cups arugula
- 1 ripe avocado, sliced
- 2 boiled eggs, halved
- 1 cup roasted pumpkin cubes (small portion to keep it keto-friendly)
- 2 tbsp olive oil
- 1 tbsp apple cider vinegar
- Salt and pepper to taste
- Optional: sprinkle of feta cheese or nuts for extra flavor

INSTRUCTIONS

1. Prepare Ingredients: Roast pumpkin cubes with olive oil, salt, and pepper at 200°C (400°F) for 20 minutes or until tender. Boil eggs to desired doneness and slice avocado.
2. Assemble Salad: In a large bowl, add arugula, roasted pumpkin cubes, avocado slices, and boiled egg halves. Drizzle with olive oil and apple cider vinegar.
3. Season with salt and pepper to taste. Optionally, add a sprinkle of feta cheese or nuts for added flavor.
4. Serve: Toss the salad gently to combine. Serve immediately.

Nutrition Facts: Calories: 250 kcal | Protein: 8 g | Carbs: 10 g | Fat: 21 g | Fiber: 7 g | Sugar: 3 g

81. Fresh Salad with Tomatoes, Avocado, and Cucumber

★★☆☆☆

10 Minutes | 0 Minutes | 4 servings

INGREDIENTS

- 1 cup cherry tomatoes, halved
- 1 avocado, sliced
- 1 cucumber, sliced
- 4 cups mixed greens (such as arugula, spinach, and lettuce)
- 2 tbsp olive oil
- 1 tbsp lemon juice
- Salt and pepper to taste

INSTRUCTIONS

1. Prepare Ingredients: Wash and halve the cherry tomatoes. Slice the avocado and cucumber. Wash and dry the mixed greens.
2. Assemble Salad: In a large bowl, combine the mixed greens, cherry tomatoes, avocado slices, and cucumber slices. Drizzle with olive oil and lemon juice. Season with salt and pepper to taste.
3. Serve: Toss the salad gently to combine all ingredients. Serve immediately.

Nutrition Facts: Calories: 200 kcal | Protein: 3 g | Carbs: 12 g | Fat: 18 g | Fiber: 7 g | Sugar: 4 g

82. Roasted Vegetables with Spicy Avocado Dip

★★☆☆☆

15 Minutes | 25 Minutes | 4 servings

INGREDIENTS

- 2 red bell peppers, sliced
- 1 zucchini, sliced
- 1 eggplant, cubed
- 1 red onion, cut into wedges
- 2 tbsp olive oil
- Salt and pepper to taste
- Fresh thyme for garnish
- Ingredients for Avocado Dip:
- 2 ripe avocados
- Juice of half a lemon
- 1 garlic clove, minced
- 1 tsp chili flakes
- Salt and pepper to taste

INSTRUCTIONS

1. Preheat the oven to 200°C (392°F) and line a baking sheet with parchment paper.
2. Spread the sliced vegetables on the prepared baking sheet, drizzle with olive oil, and season with salt and pepper. Roast for about 20-25 minutes until tender and lightly browned.
3. Meanwhile, halve the avocados, remove the pits, and scoop out the flesh.
4. In a bowl, mash the avocado with lemon juice, minced garlic, chili flakes, salt, and pepper until creamy.
5. Garnish the roasted vegetables with fresh thyme and serve with the spicy avocado dip.

Nutrition Facts: Calories: 250 kcal | Protein: 8 g | Carbs: 10 g | Fat: 21 g | Fiber: 7 g | Sugar: 3 g

83. Lime Chicken Soup

★★★☆☆

15 Minutes | 30 Minutes | 4 servings

INGREDIENTS

- 2 chicken breasts, cooked and shredded
- 6 cups chicken broth
- 2 cloves garlic, minced
- 1 small onion, diced
- 1 bell pepper, diced
- 1 jalapeno, seeded and chopped (optional)
- Juice of 2 limes
- 1 avocado, diced
- 1/4 cup fresh cilantro, chopped
- Salt and pepper to taste
- Lime wedges for serving

INSTRUCTIONS

1. Prepare Ingredients: Cook and shred the chicken breasts. Mince the garlic, dice the onion and bell pepper, and chop the jalapeno if using.
2. Cook Soup: In a large pot, heat a small amount of oil over medium heat. Add the garlic, onion, bell pepper, and jalapeno. Cook until vegetables are softened, about 5 minutes. Add the chicken broth and bring to a boil. Reduce heat and let simmer for 10 minutes.
3. Finish Soup: Add the shredded chicken and lime juice to the pot. Season with salt and pepper to taste. Simmer for an additional 5 minutes to heat through.
4. Serve: Ladle the soup into bowls. Top with diced avocado and fresh cilantro. Serve with lime wedges on the side.

Nutrition Facts : Calories: 200 kcal | Protein: 20 g | Carbs: 8 g | Fat: 10 g | Fiber: 4 g | Sugar: 2 g

84. Keto Berry Fruit Tart

★★☆☆☆

20 Minutes | 10 Minutes | 8 servings

INGREDIENTS

- For the Crust:
- 1 1/2 cups almond flour
- 1/4 cup coconut flour
- 1/4 cup powdered erythritol (or preferred keto sweetener)
- 1/4 cup melted butter
- 1 tsp vanilla extract
- A pinch of salt
- For the Filling:
- 1 cup heavy whipping cream
- 1/4 cup powdered erythritol (or preferred keto sweetener)
- 1 tsp vanilla extract
- For the Topping:
- 1/2 cup fresh raspberries
- 1/2 cup fresh blueberries
- 1/2 cup fresh strawberries, sliced
- Fresh mint leaves for garnish (optional)

INSTRUCTIONS

1. Prepare the Crust: Preheat the oven to 175°C (350°F). In a mixing bowl, combine almond flour, coconut flour, powdered erythritol, melted butter, vanilla extract, and a pinch of salt. Mix until the dough forms. Press the dough evenly into a tart pan. Bake for 10 minutes or until lightly golden. Let it cool completely.
2. Prepare the Filling: In a mixing bowl, whip the heavy cream, powdered erythritol, and vanilla extract until stiff peaks form. Spread the whipped cream mixture evenly over the cooled crust.
3. Add the Topping: Arrange the fresh berries and sliced strawberries on top of the whipped cream. Garnish with fresh mint leaves if desired.
4. Serve: Slice and serve immediately, or refrigerate until ready to serve.

Nutrition Facts: Calories: 210 kcal | Protein: 4 g | Carbs: 6 g | Fat: 19 g | Fiber: 3 g | Sugar: 3 g

DESSERT

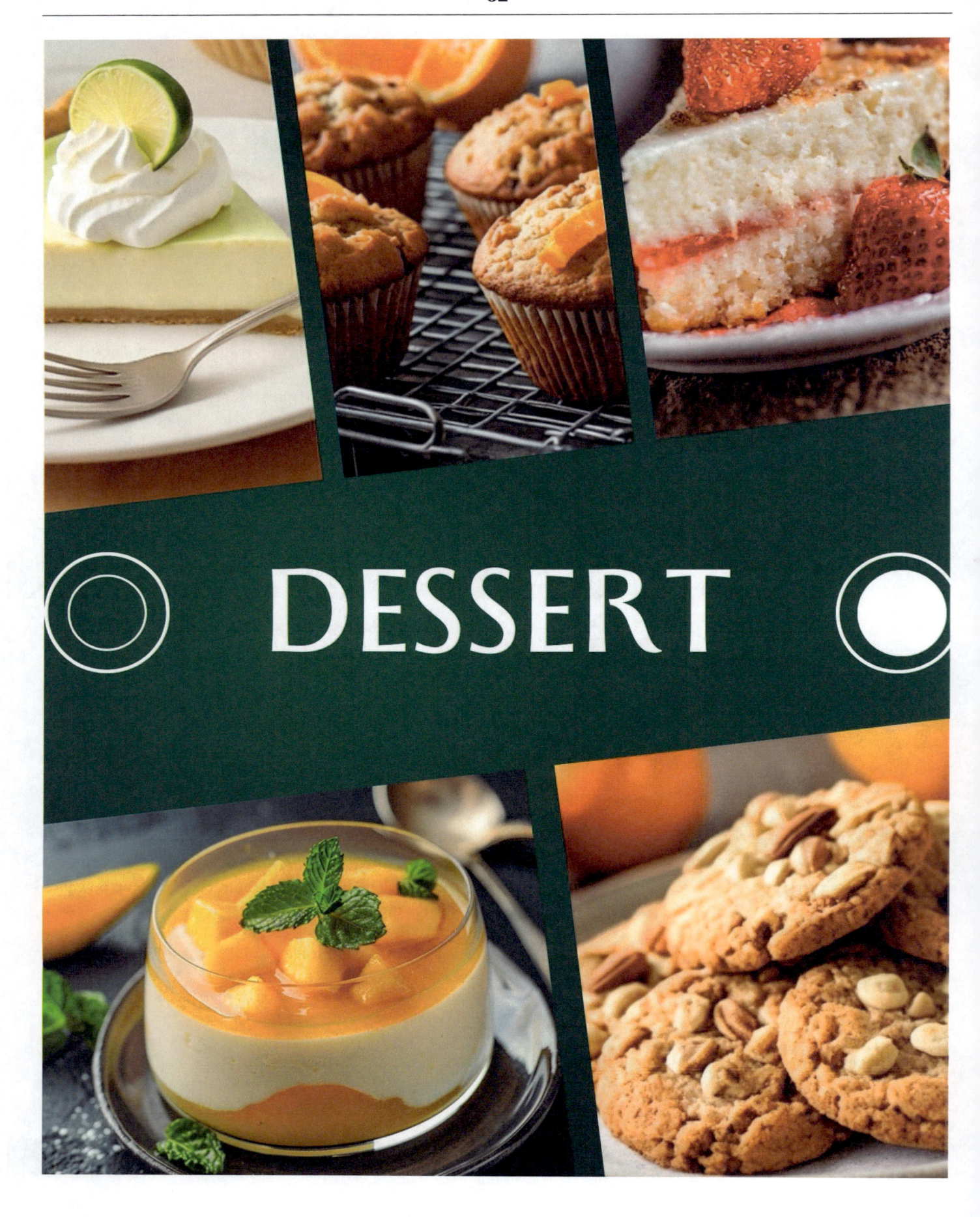

85. Layers of Creamy Coconut Pudding and Caramelized Figs

★★★☆☆

15 Minutes | 10 Minutes | 4 servings

INGREDIENTS

- For the Coconut Pudding:
- 1 can (400 ml) full-fat coconut milk
- 1/4 cup chia seeds
- 2 tbsp powdered erythritol (or preferred keto sweetener)
- 1 tsp vanilla extract
- For the Caramelized Figs:
- 8 fresh figs, halved
- 2 tbsp butter
- 1 tbsp powdered erythritol (or preferred keto sweetener)
- 1/2 tsp cinnamon

INSTRUCTIONS

1. Prepare the Coconut Pudding: In a mixing bowl, combine the coconut milk, chia seeds, powdered erythritol, and vanilla extract. Stir well and let it sit for 10 minutes, then stir again to prevent clumping. Cover and refrigerate for at least 1 hour or until it thickens to a pudding-like consistency.
2. Prepare the Caramelized Figs: In a pan over medium heat, melt the butter. Add the fig halves, cut side down, and sprinkle with powdered erythritol and cinnamon. Cook for about 5-7 minutes until the figs are caramelized and tender.
3. Assemble the Dessert: In serving glasses or bowls, layer the coconut pudding and caramelized figs. Start with a layer of coconut pudding, then add a layer of caramelized figs. Repeat until the glasses are filled, ending with a few caramelized figs on top. Dust with a little more cinnamon if desired.
4. Serve: Serve immediately or refrigerate until ready to serve.

Nutrition Facts : Calories: 250 kcal | Protein: 3 g | Carbs: 10 g | Fat: 22 g | Fiber: 5 g | Sugar: 5 g

86. Keto Yogurt with Berries and Strawberries

★★☆☆☆

5 Minutes | 0 Minutes | 1 servings

INGREDIENTS

- 1 cup plain unsweetened Greek yogurt (full-fat)
- 1/4 cup fresh strawberries, sliced
- 1/4 cup mixed berries (blueberries, raspberries, blackberries)
- 1 tbsp chia seeds (optional for added fiber)
- 1 tsp erythritol or stevia (optional, to taste)
- 1/2 tsp vanilla extract (optional)

INSTRUCTIONS

1. Prepare the Yogurt: In a bowl, mix the Greek yogurt with erythritol or stevia and vanilla extract if using. Stir until well combined.
2. Assemble the Dessert: In a glass cup, layer the yogurt at the bottom. Add a layer of mixed berries and sliced strawberries. If using chia seeds, sprinkle them on top of the berries. Add another layer of yogurt and top with the remaining berries and strawberries.
3. Serve: Serve immediately or refrigerate until ready to eat.

Nutrition Facts: Calories: 180 kcal | Protein: 10 g | Carbs: 8 g | Fat: 12 g | Fiber: 3 g | Sugar: 6 g

87. Coconut and Almond Balls

★★★★★

15 Minutes | 60 Minutes | 4 servings

INGREDIENTS
- 1/2 cup almond flour
- 1/4 cup unsweetened coconut flour
- 2 tbsp coconut oil, melted
- 2 tbsp unsweetened almond milk
- 1 tsp vanilla extract
- A pinch of salt
- Shredded coconut for rolling

INSTRUCTIONS
1. In a bowl, combine almond flour, coconut flour, coconut oil, almond milk, vanilla extract, and salt.
2. Form into small balls and roll in shredded coconut.
3. Chill in the fridge for at least 1 hour to set.

Nutrition Facts : Calories: 180 kcal | Protein: 4 g | Carbs: 8 g | Fat: 15 g | Fiber: 4 g | Sugar: 1 g

88. Avocado Chocolate Mousse

★★★★★

10 Minutes | 120 Minutes | 2 servings

INGREDIENTS
- 1 ripe avocado
- 2 tbsp unsweetened cocoa powder
- 2 tbsp low-carb sweetener (e.g., erythritol)
- 1 tsp vanilla extract
- A pinch of salt
- Fresh berries for serving

INSTRUCTIONS
1. Scoop the avocado flesh into a bowl.
2. Add cocoa powder, sweetener, vanilla extract, and salt.
3. Blend until creamy and smooth, then chill in the fridge for at least 2 hours.
4. Garnish with fresh berries before serving.

Nutrition Facts : Calories: 180 kcal | Protein: 3 g | Carbs: 10 g | Fat: 15 g | Fiber: 7 g | Sugar: 1 g

89. Vanilla Protein Bars with Almond and Coconut

★★★★☆

15 Minutes | 60 Minutes | 4 servings

INGREDIENTS
- 1 cup almond flour
- 1/4 cup unsweetened coconut flour
- 1/4 cup vanilla protein powder
- 2 tbsp coconut oil, melted
- 2 tbsp unsweetened almond milk
- 1 tsp vanilla extract
- A pinch of salt

INSTRUCTIONS
1. In a bowl, combine almond flour, coconut flour, vanilla protein powder, coconut oil, almond milk, vanilla extract, and salt.
2. Press the mixture into a flat form and chill in the fridge for at least 1 hour to set.
3. Cut into bars and enjoy!

Nutrition Facts : Calories: 160 kcal | Protein: 8 g | Carbs: 6 g | Fat: 10 g | Fiber: 4 g | Sugar: 1 g

90. Cheesecake with Fresh Berry Topping

★★★★★

20 Minutes | 240 Minutes | 8 servings

INGREDIENTS
- For the Crust:
- 1 1/2 cups almond flour
- 1/4 cup melted butter
- 2 tbsp low-carb sweetener (e.g., erythritol)
- For the Cheesecake:
- 16 oz cream cheese, softened
- 1/2 cup low-carb sweetener (e.g., erythritol)
- 1 tsp vanilla extract
- 1 cup heavy cream
- For the Topping:
- 1 cup mixed fresh berries (strawberries, blueberries, raspberries)
- 1 tbsp low-carb sweetener (e.g., erythritol)

INSTRUCTIONS
1. Prepare the Crust: In a mixing bowl, combine the almond flour, melted butter, and sweetener. Mix until the mixture resembles wet sand. Press the mixture evenly into the bottom of a springform pan. Chill in the fridge while preparing the filling.
2. Prepare the Cheesecake Filling: In a large bowl, beat the softened cream cheese with the low-carb sweetener until smooth and creamy. Add the vanilla extract and heavy cream, and continue to beat until the mixture is well combined and smooth.
3. Assemble the Cheesecake: Pour the cheesecake filling over the prepared crust, smoothing the top with a spatula. Chill in the fridge for at least 4 hours, or until the cheesecake is set.
4. Prepare the Berry Topping: In a small bowl, mix the fresh berries with the sweetener. Let sit for a few minutes to macerate.
5. Serve: Once the cheesecake is set, remove it from the springform pan. Top with the fresh berry mixture just before serving.

Nutrition Facts : Calories: 320 kcal | Protein: 5 g | Carbs: 7 g | Fat: 30 g | Fiber: 3 g | Sugar: 3 g

91. Strawberry Syrup Cake

★★★★☆

20 Minutes | 40 Minutes | 8 servings

INGREDIENTS
- 1 1/2 cups almond flour
- 1/4 cup coconut flour
- 1/2 cup low-carb sweetener (e.g., erythritol)
- 1 tsp baking powder
- 1/4 tsp salt
- 4 large eggs
- 1/2 cup unsweetened almond milk
- 1/4 cup melted butter
- 1 tsp vanilla extract
- 1 cup fresh strawberries, hulled and chopped
- 2 tbsp low-carb sweetener (e.g., erythritol)
- 1/2 cup water

INSTRUCTIONS
1. Prepare the Cake: Preheat the oven to 175°C (350°F) and grease a round cake pan. In a large bowl, combine the almond flour, coconut flour, sweetener, baking powder, and salt. In another bowl, whisk together the eggs, almond milk, melted butter, and vanilla extract. Add the wet ingredients to the dry ingredients and mix until well combined. Pour the batter into the prepared cake pan and smooth the top with a spatula. Bake for 35-40 minutes, or until a toothpick inserted into the center comes out clean. Allow the cake to cool in the pan for 10 minutes, then transfer to a wire rack to cool completely.
2. Prepare the Strawberry Syrup: In a small saucepan, combine the chopped strawberries, sweetener, and water. Bring to a boil over medium heat, then reduce to a simmer and cook for 10-15 minutes, or until the strawberries are soft and the syrup has thickened slightly. Remove from heat and let cool.
3. Serve: Slice the cooled cake and serve with a drizzle of strawberry syrup and fresh strawberries on top.

Nutrition Facts : Calories: 250 kcal | Protein: 6 g | Carbs: 8 g | Fat: 21 g | Fiber: 4 g | Sugar: 3 g

92. Sugar-Free Coconut Almond Cookies

★★★☆☆

15 Minutes | 15 Minutes | 8 servings

INGREDIENTS
- 1 cup almond flour
- 1/2 cup unsweetened coconut flour
- 1/4 cup shredded coconut
- 1/4 cup coconut oil, melted
- 2 tbsp low-carb sweetener (e.g., erythritol)
- 1 tsp vanilla extract
- 1/2 tsp baking powder
- A pinch of salt

INSTRUCTIONS
1. Preheat the oven to 180°C (356°F) and line a baking sheet with parchment paper.
2. In a bowl, combine almond flour, coconut flour, shredded coconut, coconut oil, sweetener, vanilla extract, baking powder, and salt.
3. Form small dough balls and place them on the baking sheet.
4. Bake for 15 minutes until golden brown.
5. Cool before serving.

Nutrition Facts: Calories: 180 kcal | Protein: 4 g | Carbs: 6 g | Fat: 15 g | Fiber: 4 g | Sugar: 1 g

93. Lemon Coconut Tarts

★★★★☆

20 Minutes | 120 Minutes | 4 servings

INSTRUCTIONS

1. In a bowl, combine shredded coconut, coconut flour, lemon juice, lemon zest, coconut oil, sweetener, and salt.
2. Press the mixture into small tart molds and set in the fridge.
3. Chill for at least 2 hours before serving.

INGREDIENTS

- 1 cup unsweetened shredded coconut
- 1/4 cup unsweetened coconut flour
- Juice and zest of 1 lemon
- 2 tbsp coconut oil, melted
- 2 tbsp low-carb sweetener (e.g., erythritol)
- A pinch of salt

Nutrition Facts: Calories: 160 kcal | Protein: 2 g | Carbs: 6 g | Fat: 12 g | Fiber: 3 g | Sugar: 1 g

94. Buckwheat Pudding with Whipped Cream

★★★★☆

15 Minutes | 25 Minutes | 4 servings

INSTRUCTIONS

1. Prepare the Pudding: Rinse the buckwheat groats thoroughly under cold water. In a medium saucepan, combine the buckwheat groats and almond milk. Bring to a boil over medium heat, then reduce to a simmer. Cook for 20-25 minutes, stirring occasionally, until the buckwheat is tender and the mixture has thickened. Stir in the sweetener, vanilla extract, and ground cinnamon. Remove from heat and let cool slightly. Transfer the pudding to serving bowls and chill in the refrigerator for at least 1 hour.
2. Prepare the Whipped Cream: In a chilled bowl, beat the heavy cream with an electric mixer until soft peaks form. Add the sweetener and vanilla extract, then continue beating until stiff peaks form.
3. Serve: Top each serving of buckwheat pudding with a dollop of whipped cream. Sprinkle with ground cinnamon for garnish.

INGREDIENTS

- For the Pudding:
    - 1/2 cup buckwheat groats
    - 2 cups unsweetened almond milk
    - 2 tbsp low-carb sweetener (e.g., erythritol)
    - 1 tsp vanilla extract
    - 1/4 tsp ground cinnamon
- For the Whipped Cream:
    - 1/2 cup heavy cream
    - 1 tbsp low-carb sweetener (e.g., erythritol)
    - 1/2 tsp vanilla extract
- For Garnish:
    - A sprinkling of ground cinnamon

Nutrition Facts: Calories: 180 kcal | Protein: 4 g | Carbs: 14 g | Fat: 12 g | Fiber: 3 g | Sugar: 2 g

95. Tartlets with Blueberries

★★★★☆

⏲ 20 Minutes 🍳 15 Minutes 🍴 6 servings

INGREDIENTS

- For the Crust:
- 1 cup almond flour
- 2 tbsp coconut flour
- 2 tbsp unsweetened shredded coconut
- 1/4 cup melted coconut oil
- 2 tbsp low-carb sweetener (e.g., erythritol)
- 1/2 tsp vanilla extract
- A pinch of salt
- For the Filling:
- 1 cup fresh blueberries
- 1/2 cup unsweetened coconut cream
- 2 tbsp low-carb sweetener (e.g., erythritol)
- 1 tsp lemon zest
- 1/2 tsp vanilla extract
- For Garnish:
- Fresh blueberries
- Mint leaves

INSTRUCTIONS

1. Prepare the Crust: Preheat the oven to 175°C (350°F). In a mixing bowl, combine almond flour, coconut flour, shredded coconut, melted coconut oil, sweetener, vanilla extract, and a pinch of salt. Mix until a dough forms. Press the dough evenly into tartlet molds, making sure to cover the bottoms and sides. Bake for 10-15 minutes or until the crusts are golden brown. Remove from the oven and let cool completely.
2. Prepare the Filling: In a bowl, whisk together the coconut cream, sweetener, lemon zest, and vanilla extract until smooth. Gently fold in the blueberries.
3. Assemble the Tartlets: Spoon the blueberry filling into the cooled tartlet crusts. Chill in the refrigerator for at least 1 hour to set.
4. Serve: Garnish with fresh blueberries and mint leaves before serving.

Nutrition Facts : Calories: 220 kcal | Protein: 4 g | Carbs: 10 g | Fat: 18 g | Fiber: 5 g | Sugar: 3 g

96. Lemon Cheesecake Slice with Blueberry and Mint Garnish

★★★★☆

⏲ 20 Minutes 🍳 45 Minutes 🍴 8 servings

INGREDIENTS

- 1 cup almond flour
- 2 tbsp coconut flour
- 1/4 cup melted coconut oil
- 2 tbsp low-carb sweetener (e.g., erythritol)
- 1/2 tsp vanilla extract
- A pinch of salt
- 16 oz (450 g) cream cheese, softened
- 3/4 cup low-carb sweetener (e.g., erythritol)
- 3 large eggs
- 1/4 cup fresh lemon juice
- 1 tbsp lemon zest
- 1 tsp vanilla extract
- 1/4 cup sour cream
- Fresh blueberries
- Fresh mint leaves

INSTRUCTIONS

1. Prepare the Crust: Preheat the oven to 175°C (350°F). In a mixing bowl, combine almond flour, coconut flour, melted coconut oil, sweetener, vanilla extract, and a pinch of salt. Mix until a dough forms. Press the dough evenly into the bottom of a 9-inch springform pan. Bake for 10-12 minutes or until the crust is lightly golden. Remove from the oven and let cool.
2. Prepare the Cheesecake Filling: In a large mixing bowl, beat the cream cheese and sweetener until smooth. Add the eggs one at a time, beating well after each addition. Mix in the lemon juice, lemon zest, and vanilla extract. Fold in the sour cream until well combined.
3. Bake the Cheesecake: Pour the cheesecake filling over the cooled crust in the springform pan. Bake in the preheated oven for 45-50 minutes, or until the center is set and the edges are lightly browned. Turn off the oven and let the cheesecake cool in the oven with the door slightly open for about 1 hour. Remove from the oven and refrigerate for at least 4 hours, or overnight.
4. Serve: Before serving, garnish each slice with fresh blueberries and mint leaves.

Nutrition Facts : Calories: 320 kcal | Protein: 8 g | Carbs: 6 g | Fat: 30 g | Fiber: 2 g | Sugar: 3 g

97. Vegan Raspberry Chocolate Bark

★★★★☆

⏱ 10 Minutes   🍳 30 Minutes   🍴 12 servings

INGREDIENTS

- 1 cup dark chocolate chips (vegan)
- 1/4 cup freeze-dried raspberries
- 1/4 cup chopped almonds
- 1/4 cup shredded coconut

INSTRUCTIONS

1. Melt dark chocolate chips in a double boiler or microwave until smooth.
2. Spread melted chocolate on a parchment-lined baking sheet.
3. Sprinkle with freeze-dried raspberries, chopped almonds, and shredded coconut.
4. Refrigerate for 30 minutes or until set.
5. Break into pieces and serve.

Nutrition Facts: Calories: 100 kcal | Protein: 2 g | Carbs: 10 g | Fat: 7 g | Fiber: 2 g | Sugar: 6 g

98. Homemade Oatmeal Cookies with Cranberries and Nuts

★★★★☆

⏱ 20 Minutes   🍳 45 Minutes   🍴 8 servings

INSTRUCTIONS

1. **Preheat the Oven:** Preheat the oven to 175°C (350°F). Line a baking sheet with parchment paper.
2. **Prepare the Dough:** In a large mixing bowl, combine almond flour, coconut flour, shredded coconut, and low-carb sweetener. Mix well. Add the melted coconut oil, eggs, and vanilla extract. Mix until a dough forms. Stir in the baking soda, ground cinnamon, and salt until well combined. Fold in the dried cranberries and chopped nuts.
3. **Form the Cookies:** Using a spoon or cookie scoop, drop dough onto the prepared baking sheet, spacing them about 2 inches apart. Flatten each cookie slightly with the back of the spoon.
4. **Bake the Cookies:** Bake in the preheated oven for 10-12 minutes, or until the edges are golden brown Remove from the oven and let the cookies cool on the baking sheet for 5 minutes before transferring them to a wire rack to cool completely.
5. **Serve:** Enjoy the cookies as a snack or dessert.

INGREDIENTS

- 1 cup almond flour
- 1/2 cup coconut flour
- 1/2 cup unsweetened shredded coconut
- 1/2 cup low-carb sweetener (e.g., erythritol)
- 1/4 cup coconut oil, melted
- 2 large eggs
- 1 tsp vanilla extract
- 1/2 tsp baking soda
- 1/2 tsp ground cinnamon
- 1/4 tsp salt
- 1/2 cup dried cranberries (unsweetened)
- 1/2 cup chopped nuts (e.g., walnuts, pecans)

Nutrition Facts: Calories: 90 kcal | Protein: 2 g | Carbs: 6 g | Fat: 7 g | Fiber: 2 g | Sugar: 1 g

99. Vegan Coconut Macaroons

★★★★☆

10 Minutes | **20 Minutes** | **16 servings**

INGREDIENTS

- 2 cups shredded coconut
- 1/4 cup coconut flour
- 1/4 cup maple syrup
- 1/4 cup coconut oil, melted
- 1 tsp vanilla extract
- Pinch of salt

INSTRUCTIONS

1. Preheat the oven to 160 degrees Celsius.
2. In a bowl, mix shredded coconut, coconut flour, maple syrup, melted coconut oil, vanilla extract, and salt.
3. Form small balls and place on a lined baking sheet.
4. Bake for 20 minutes or until golden brown.
5. Let cool before serving.

Nutrition Facts : Calories: 90 kcal | Protein: 1 g | Carbs: 7 g | Fat: 7 g | Fiber: 2 g | Sugar: 4 g

100. Lemon Muffin

★★★★☆

20 Minutes | **45 Minutes** | **8 servings**

INGREDIENTS

- 2 cups almond flour
- 1/2 cup sugar
- 1 teaspoon baking powder
- 1/4 cup olive oil
- 2 eggs
- Juice and zest of 1 lemon
- 1/4 cup almond milk

INSTRUCTIONS

1. Preheat the oven to 350°F (175°C). Line a muffin tin with paper liners.
2. In a bowl, mix together the almond flour, sugar, and baking powder.
3. In another bowl, whisk the olive oil, eggs, lemon juice, lemon zest, and almond milk.
4. Combine the wet and dry ingredients and mix until smooth.
5. Divide the batter evenly among the muffin cups.
6. Bake for 20 minutes, or until a toothpick inserted into the center comes out clean.
7. Let cool before serving.

Nutritional : Calories: 275 kcal | Protein: 8 g | Carbohydrates: 20 g | Fat: 20 g | Fiber: 3 g | Sugar: 12 g

28-Day Meal plan

Day	Breakfast	Lunch	Dinner	Snacks
1	1. Spinach-Feta Omelet	51. Baked Scallops with Herb Butter	70. Barbecue Pork Ribs	84. Keto Berry Fruit Tart
2	2. Avocado Egg Boats with Bacon	48. Pink Salmon Steak Fried and Salad	64. Chicken with Lemon Slices	87. Coconut and Almond Balls
3	3. Keto Frittata with Mushrooms, Zucchini, and Cheese	40. Crispy Fried Shrimp with Avocado Dip	69. Steak with Green Garnish	89. Vanilla Protein Bars with Almond and Coconut
4	4. Keto Baked Pumpkin Slices with Herbs and Garlic	42. Shrimps and Avocado Salad with Soft Fried Egg	62. Lamb Chops with Pesto Sauce	85. Layers of Creamy Coconut Pudding and Caramelized Figs
5	5. Keto Toast with Salmon, Avocado, Poached Egg, and Cheese	49. Fried Broccoli with Garlic and Shrimp	65. Grilled Chicken Breast and Spinach Salad with Avocado, Tomatoes, and Sesame Seeds	91. Strawberry Syrup Cake
6	6. Fried Eggs with Broccoli and Cheese	41. Baked Perch with Herb Crust	63. Grilled Meat with Blueberry Sauce	86. Keto Yogurt with Berries and Strawberries
7	7. Keto Toasts with Ricotta, Egg, Cucumber, and Black Sesame	47. Steamed Cod with Tomatoes and Olives	67. Keto Salad with Chicken Meat Sous Vide, Tomatoes, Cucumbers, and Avocado	92. Sugar-Free Coconut Almond Cookies
8	8. Asparagus with Prosciutto, Avocado, and Fried Eggs	39. Salmon Fish Fillet with Fresh Salad and Avocado	60. Grilled Steak and Pear Salad with Blue Cheese	88. Avocado Chocolate Mousse
9	9. Fried Eggs with Vegetables	50. Pan-Fried Tuna with Sesame Seeds	66. Baked Scallops with Herb Butter	93. Lemon Coconut Tarts
10	10. Keto Yogurt with Chocolate Pieces and Crumbs	46. Salmon Fillet with Broccoli and Almond Crust	61. Chicken with Onions, Capers, and Lemon Zest	94. Buckwheat Pudding with Whipped Cream

11	11. Low-Carb Blueberry Smoothie	43. Tuna Salad with Quail Eggs, Lettuce, Red Onion, and Cucumbers	70. Barbecue Pork Ribs	95. Tartlets with Blueberries
12	12. Keto Berry Fruit Smoothie	38. Baked Salmon with Asparagus and Tomatoes	72. Fresh Chicken Salad with Seasonings	96. Lemon Cheesecake Slice with Blueberry and Mint Garnish
13	13. Green Smoothie with Spinach and Fresh Green Vegetables	55. Salmon Cooked with Asparagus	68. Chicken Salad with Avocado, Spinach, and Blueberries	97. Vegan Raspberry Chocolate Bark
14	14. Avocado Keto Chocolate Pudding	45. Japanese Traditional Salad with Grilled Ahi Tuna and Sesame	73. Meatballs with Vegetables	98. Homemade Oatmeal Cookies with Cranberries and Nuts
15	1. Spinach-Feta Omelet	54. Avocado Oil-Based Aioli Sauce	75. Summer Salad with Arugula, Strawberry, and Nuts	84. Keto Berry Fruit Tart
16	2. Avocado Egg Boats with Bacon	48. Pink Salmon Steak Fried and Salad	74. Meatballs with Tomato Sauce and Basil Garnish	87. Coconut and Almond Balls
17	3. Keto Frittata with Mushrooms, Zucchini, and Cheese	40. Crispy Fried Shrimp with Avocado Dip	69. Steak with Green Garnish	89. Vanilla Protein Bars with Almond and Coconut
18	4. Keto Baked Pumpkin Slices with Herbs and Garlic	42. Shrimps and Avocado Salad with Soft Fried Egg	62. Lamb Chops with Pesto Sauce	85. Layers of Creamy Coconut Pudding and Caramelized Figs
19	5. Keto Toast with Salmon, Avocado, Poached Egg, and Cheese	49. Fried Broccoli with Garlic and Shrimp	65. Grilled Chicken Breast and Spinach Salad with Avocado, Tomatoes, and Sesame Seeds	91. Strawberry Syrup Cake
20	6. Fried Eggs with Broccoli and Cheese	41. Baked Perch with Herb Crust	63. Grilled Meat with Blueberry Sauce	86. Keto Yogurt with Berries and Strawberries
21	7. Keto Toasts with Ricotta, Egg, Cucumber, and Black Sesame	47. Steamed Cod with Tomatoes and Olives	67. Keto Salad with Chicken Meat Sous Vide, Tomatoes, Cucumbers, and Avocado	92. Sugar-Free Coconut Almond Cookies

22	8. Asparagus with Prosciutto, Avocado, and Fried Eggs	39. Salmon Fish Fillet with Fresh Salad and Avocado	60. Grilled Steak and Pear Salad with Blue Cheese	88. Avocado Chocolate Mousse
23	9. Fried Eggs with Vegetables	50. Pan-Fried Tuna with Sesame Seeds	66. Baked Scallops with Herb Butter	93. Lemon Coconut Tarts
24	10. Keto Yogurt with Chocolate Pieces and Crumbs	46. Salmon Fillet with Broccoli and Almond Crust	61. Chicken with Onions, Capers, and Lemon Zest	94. Buckwheat Pudding with Whipped Cream
25	11. Low-Carb Blueberry Smoothie	43. Tuna Salad with Quail Eggs, Lettuce, Red Onion, and Cucumbers	70. Barbecue Pork Ribs	95. Tartlets with Blueberries
26	12. Keto Berry Fruit Smoothie	38. Baked Salmon with Asparagus and Tomatoes	72. Fresh Chicken Salad with Seasonings	96. Lemon Cheesecake Slice with Blueberry and Mint Garnish
27	13. Green Smoothie with Spinach and Fresh Green Vegetables	55. Salmon Cooked with Asparagus	68. Chicken Salad with Avocado, Spinach, and Blueberries	97. Vegan Raspberry Chocolate Bark
28	14. Avocado Keto Chocolate Pudding	45. Japanese Traditional Salad with Grilled Ahi Tuna and Sesame	73. Meatballs with Vegetables	98. Homemade Oatmeal Cookies with Cranberries and Nuts

2 Bonuses:

7 Secrets for Success with the Keto Diet
Video recipes with step-by-step explanations

Made in United States
Troutdale, OR
02/26/2025